The Reach of the State

Vivienne Shue

The Reach of the State

Sketches of the Chinese Body Politic

STANFORD UNIVERSITY PRESS

STANFORD, CALIFORNIA

Stanford University Press
Stanford, California
© 1988 by the Board of Trustees of the
Leland Stanford Junior University
Printed in the United States of America

CIP data appear at the end of the book

FOR HENRY

Acknowledgments

The first drafts of the essays included here were all written during the early 1980s. That was a time of profound metamorphosis and uncertainty in China, when it was even more difficult than it usually is for serious observers to comment thoughtfully on contemporary Chinese affairs. Evidence was mounting month by month that what most scholars (myself included) would previously have regarded as practically unthinkable changes were indeed under way in China's post-Mao economy and polity. The best and the wisest among us became not only less sure of *what* to think about the nature of Chinese political life, but also less sure even of *how* to think about it. Writing these essays helped me through that process of rethinking. If reading them should now prove to have any value at all for others, it will be because I was fortunate enough to have both some time free to read and write during those crucial years and some generous and committed colleagues with whom to share ideas. Acknowledgment of those professional and personal debts to institutions and friends is an obligation I discharge here with genuine pleasure and sincerest thanks to all.

I am grateful to both Jim Scott and Marc Blecher for detailed critical readings of earlier versions of Chapters Two, Three, and Four. In Chapters Three and Four, readers will find scattered references to a series of interviews I carried out in Hong Kong in 1978. That project, supported by a Social

Science Research Council postdoctoral grant, also owes much to the friendship of Marc Blecher. Generously sharing informants, tapes, notes, and many hours of conversation at the Universities Service Centre, Marc essentially showed me the ropes of émigré interviewing. Over the intervening years I have found it very valuable to return again and again to those carefully compiled interview transcripts to remind myself of how the problems of the Chinese countryside appeared to us—and to our informants—then.

Chapter Two was originally presented as a paper at the American Political Science Association meetings in 1981, and it was thanks to a Yale University Junior Faculty Fellowship in 1980–81 that I had time to prepare it. Chapter Three was thoroughly revised several times, and Chapter Four was first written during 1984–85, with support from the Wang Institute of Graduate Studies and the Institute for Advanced Study in Princeton. The intellectual mix among members and fellows, along with the peace and hospitality provided by the Institute, made it a splendid environment in which to draw my various threads of thought together.

Since Chapter Three took me deeply into periods (and scholarly debates) in Chinese history where political scientists and other outsiders tend wisely to fear to tread, I made a point of seeking extra help with the research. For their many constructive criticisms and suggestions, I am most grateful to Paul Cohen, Evelyn Rawski, Jonathan Spence, Mary Rankin, Sherman Cochran, and Willard Peterson. Present readers may be assured that they have been spared entanglement in various confusions and delusions thanks to the patient corrections and queries of these scholars even if, in the end, I have proved unable to do justice to all the valid concerns they raised. Revision of this chapter also benefited substantially from thoughtful readings by Benedict Anderson, Michel Oksenberg, and Mark Selden. And I would like to thank also Benjamin Schwartz, Richard Baum, Susan Shirk, and Perry Link for their individual expressions of encouragement when this paper was first presented at a conference sponsored by the Joint Committee on Chinese Studies in Harwichport, Massachusetts, in June 1984.

My appreciation also to three Cornell colleagues: Peter Katzenstein has saved readers of Chapters One and Four from a certain amount of tedium and tendentiousness; Martin Shefter and Sidney Tarrow have never failed to offer me encouragement and good advice about this little volume.

In addition, I am pleased to record my very special thanks to Daniel Kelliher, whose work has taught me so much over the past several years.

And finally, I am much indebted to Muriel Bell, at Stanford University Press, for lending her enthusiasm and editorial expertise to the process of making these essays into a book.

None of these institutions or individuals is, in the least, to be thought responsible for what I have written here, of course. For better or worse, all arguments, judgments, and expressions of opinion are mine alone.

V.B.S.

Contents

The Reach of the State

Introduction

These are experimental essays. Their concerns are more critical and conceptual than empirical. They are the imperfect artifacts of several years of somewhat fitful searching for an approach to the study of contemporary Chinese political life that would be both sufficiently disciplined to be practiced with care and sufficiently flexible to encompass all the evidence of flux and change that we have lately witnessed.

In essence, these are essays about how to think about the Chinese state: about its complex structures, roles, and capacities; about its interrelations with Chinese society as a whole and with rural social organization in particular; and most especially about the process of its evolution, the patterns of change we can discern not only in its forms and functions but also in its most fundamental ethos. The effort to develop simultaneously more refined and more dynamic ways of thinking about these problems, however uncertainly it is executed in these essays, stemmed initially from nagging dissatisfaction with the available models and approaches to studying the Chinese polity that have filled the literature. If the Maoist language of "class struggle and capitalist restoration" seemed hollow by the 1980s, so too did the intra-elite power struggle models still widely clung to in the West. And though East European revisionist theorists had much of interest to teach us about socialist states and societies, their dilemmas of govern-

ment had crystallized in social formations so thoroughly unlike the Chinese that true parallels, lessons, and comparisons
were, sadly, very scarce. All my own earlier empirical investigations had left me with a working knowledge of the politics
of rural China that made the *processes* involved seem far
more intricate and multifaceted, more subtle and variable,
more full of failures and frustrations, inefficiencies and mis-
calculations, half-truths and double-entendres than the available models of China's state, society, and politics were able
comfortably to accommodate. The goal, then, was to find a
way of thinking about the Chinese polity, and a research
method, that would put the explanation of *process* at the center of the work, while leaving plenty of room for close examination of that complex embroidery of forces, pushing and
pulling, in which the processes under study were embedded
and emerging.

It may as well be confessed from the outset, however, that
as the four essays here were each originally hammered into
shape, these nobler theoretical and methodological goals
were not always held sharply in view. Each was conceived
with a more modest and bounded immediate purpose. And it
will do these pieces no injustice to point out further that, at
their core, they all rest on the elaboration of just one borrowed concept . . . and one hunch.

My hunch was that many of the seemingly special complexities and unusual syndromes that distinguished the Chinese
experience with socialism, causing it to deviate from the clean
lines laid down in various models, must have had something
to do with the vastness of the peasant social base, with the
sheer weight of the peasantry in the overall constitution of the
polity. I would therefore focus my work on the dynamics of
politics in the countryside, and on the shifting place of the
peasantry in the evolving socialist polity.

The borrowed concept was the somewhat cartographic notion that a parcelized substructure, a "cellular" pattern, characterized the organization of the Chinese peasant economy

and society. Even as late as the early 1980s, if we had wanted to sketch the skeleton of social, economic, or political life in rural China, we would probably have produced something resembling an enormous honeycomb of small, similar, connected yet more or less fully bounded cells of mostly inward-regarding activity. This persistence, thirty years after the socialist revolution, of a cell-like formation, of a marked quality of boundedness and discreteness in the communities where peasants lived, worked, and participated in public life, seemed very striking. It seemed, also, quite likely to turn out to be a crucial element in the analysis of Chinese state-society relations and patterns of politics.

It was, of course, G. William Skinner's important early work on traditional Chinese marketing systems that had first given currency to the idea of a cellular pattern of organization of the rural periphery.[1] But Skinner had used this insight to emphasize not the discreteness of the rural cells he sketched, but rather the means of their linkage into quite far-flung networks, which, through commerce and social intercourse, brought about more than a modicum of integration between urban and rural socioeconomy before the revolution.

Audrey Donnithorne later revived the concept of cellularity to characterize what she saw as the relative fragmentation of the Chinese economy in the wake of the Cultural Revolution's attacks on the central and provincial party/state bureaucracies.[2] But Nicholas Lardy, who had been closely studying the organization and management of the economy *before* the Cultural Revolution, had found little evidence of entrenched cellularity in the 1950s, and had emphasized, on the contrary, the relatively high degree of centralized state control over planning and finance in that era.[3] If Donnithorne and Lardy were both correct, then clearly there had been a change—an intensification of a tendency, perhaps—toward greater cellularity in the economic structure over time.

In any case, the possibility that there was some kind of latent pattern or tendency toward cellularity built into the peasant economic and social substructure, which might become more or less prominent under varying circumstances, seemed worth pursuing. It would be worth pursuing, beyond the confines of these interesting studies in economics and economic anthropology, for its political ramifications—for what it might have to tell us about the changing shape of the Chinese polity. In one way or another, all four of these essays are ground-clearing exercises for that sustained theoretical and empirical pursuit.

The first essay was initially inspired by the recent resurgence, in Western journalism and scholarship, of totalitarian imagery to describe the Chinese polity under Mao. Just when we thought the "totalitarian model" had finally been consigned to the crammed dustbin of intellectual history, Chinese and Western analysts alike began referring (with apparent seriousness) to 1970s ultra-leftism as a period of "fascist dictatorship," and to the Cultural Revolution itself as a "holocaust of terror." In speaking against this sad retrogression to the simplisticism of an earlier time, the essay also documents some of the progress, some of the conceptual distance traveled, by Western social scientists in their studies of Chinese politics over the last thirty years. A number of more sophisticated approaches are briefly considered, their contributions evaluated, and their shortcomings criticized. The essay concludes with a recommendation of a general approach and method we might all consider aiming for in present studies of the Chinese polity. It is an approach that puts the analysis of *process* at the center of the research effort and traces the mutually conditioning interactions among elements in the polity that tend more commonly to be dichotomized into abstractions like "state and society," "structure and culture." I label this approach the study of the *social intertexture* of Chinese politics, and suggest a method of research and writing to accompany it that involves the analyst in continually juxtaposing the finest of complex local detail with the most sweeping of discernible social trends and patterns. It is just one possible way of underscoring in our work that political evolution occurs simultaneously along many different dimensions and at different paces. With uneven success, the three remaining essays illustrate and elaborate this general approach.

The second essay offers a preliminary sketch of several different dimensions along which we might observe and measure the processes of political evolution. It adopts some of the trappings of a center-periphery approach and employs the language of social integration theory in order to make certain contrasts (for the Chinese case only) with the sequential assumptions and models of "modernization" theories. It plots an argument (or more precisely, a hypothesis for empirical investigation) that state penetration and control of rural society under Mao was more uneven and less complete than is often imagined by scholars—or for that matter by Mao Zedong's political friends and enemies. In my present view, this essay does not succeed in overcoming a certain static orientation to the problem. But it does clarify and elaborate the notion of cellularity or parcelization of the peasant periphery. It suggests, further, why the roles and behaviors of local cadres, working at the lively intersection of state structure and village society, may merit special attention. And it points toward a more dynamic understanding of the mutually conditioning interactions that may constantly be taking place between elements of state and society, by emphasizing not only the ways in which the party/state penetrated and impinged on rural social life under Mao, but also the ways in which peasant society left its imprint on contemporary Chinese state organization and routines.

The third essay adopts a very different approach in order to explore further the many crucial roles played by rural local cadres in mediating the interrelations of state and society under Mao. It takes a historical and comparative long view in order to contrast patterns of statemaking and of state-society interactions in the West with those of imperial China. It then sets up a comparison of some of the social and political roles of China's traditional local gentry with those of her latter-day local elites, the postrevolutionary rural cadres. This essay again speculates on some of the causes and the political consequences of the persistence of the parcelized pattern of rural socioeconomic organization, linking this pattern to an appreciation of certain de facto limitations on the everyday reach of the state into the peasant periphery under Mao. This provides a somewhat unusual vantage point from which to assess the full import of the post-Mao rural reforms and their implications for the course of state-society relations in China as the goal of "modernization" is pursued. Unlike most analysts, who tend to see the reforms of the Deng era as efforts essentially to roll back the power and the penetration of the state in social life, I suggest here that the rationalizing thrust of the reforms, when coupled with the deliberate effort to erase or transcend the old cellularity of "backward" peasant economy and society, may ultimately serve state-strengthening, even statist, ends.

This essay illustrates the method, alluded to above, of juxtaposing fine local knowledge and detail against the most sweeping of trends and grand designs that we are able to perceive in history. And the comparative-historical approach of this chapter does achieve greater range and richness of explanation than the center-periphery or social integration language of the preceding essay. Or so it seems to me. But it does not break away completely from a static standpoint. In the final analysis, the method here resembles more the comparison of snapshots across time than a true study of process itself.

The final essay is an outline of how a genuine study of the *social intertexture* of China's evolving polity might proceed. The time period considered is greatly narrowed to cover only postrevolutionary developments. In this narrative sketch, elements of "state" and "society," "structure" and "culture," "fine detail" and "grand design" are repeatedly juxtaposed to help interpret and explain the gradually intensifying parcelization of the polity under Mao. The significance of this fundamental structural evolution, in the kinds of limitations it placed on state capacity and control in the countryside, is then further clarified in the light of simultaneous changes in popular social ideals and cadres' behavioral norms, which had been emerging in response to the political campaigns of the 1960s and '70s. The interweaving of all these elements reveals a set of common patterns of compromise and power division that worked together to reduce central state authority and to erode its efficacy in the countryside. What authority the central party/state loudly proclaimed, and what it settled for, were frequently very far apart during Mao's last years. The honeycomb polity may have been resilient, but it was also downright cumbersome, and not always responsive to central direction. Thus, the still-unfolding rural reforms of the post-Mao period are placed again in a perspective that suggests a deep irony to their impact. Given the corrosion of authority and the fragmentation of power in the polity before Mao's death, the structural reforms and the substitute social ideals of the Deng Xiaoping coalition may serve not so much to weaken as to repackage and enhance governmental authority and efficacy, even as it is claimed that their intent is to shorten the greedy reach of the state and to loosen its grip on the peasantry.

The last essay brings together, then, most of the important theoretical lessons and empirical themes raised in the others. It remains however, an outline, a sketch of an argument, like the other essays here. To fill in the finer details and apply the colors to this political mural must be the tasks of another volume.

One

State, Society, and Politics under Mao

Theory and Irony in the Study of Contemporary China

So let us stop playing the "generation game." If we consider Stalinism in its second sense, as a set of institutional forms, practices, abstracted theories, and dominative attitudes, then the "post-Stalinist generation" has not yet been born. Stalinism, in this sense, gave to us the agenda of the present, and its forms and modes "weigh like an alp" on the brains of the living. And the living (never mind which generation) need their combined strength to shift that alp. If you have had an alp on your mind, you will know that it is not removed by a theoretical shrug of the shoulders. E. P. THOMPSON

*R*ecent years have witnessed a significant readjustment in the complex of relationships between state and society in China. How permanent current trends may turn out to be, and how likely they are actually to contribute to an altered political future for the Chinese people, are matters still wide open to speculation and doubt among students of Chinese affairs. Yet few today would find it possible to dispute that *something* fundamental in the nature of Chinese state-society relations is in the midst of rapid reorientation and qualitative change.

Unfortunately, we find ourselves poorly prepared for the scholarly challenge attendant on this state of affairs. Because we lack a fruitful repertoire of theoretical concepts and empirical analyses of state-society relations in the Maoist *past*, we find it difficult to generate the vocabulary we need to describe the nature and explain the significance of the reordering that seems so palpable in the *present*. With few exceptions, scholars of the 1950s, '60s and '70s devoted little attention to the analysis of state power, and even less to the nature of state-society relationships in Mao's China.[1] Strange as this may seem in the 1980s, when "regulating the relation between state and society" appears high on the reformists' agenda in Beijing, and when "state theory" is again popular in the wider profession of political science, the reasons for our present theoretical dilemma are not far to seek.

A Kaleidoscope of Approaches

In the early 1950s, as the new party/state was consolidating its rule over the mainland, ready-made categories for understanding Chinese affairs already held the field in Western social science. The theory of "totalitarianism"—the superpenetration of the state into and overriding all aspects of individual and social life—complete with its attached concepts of the cult of the charismatic leader, social atomization, brainwashing, and terror, provided the initial lenses through which scholars viewed the Chinese experiment and compared it with the experience of "satellites" and socialist states in other parts of the world. In the United States, under the baleful influence of McCarthyite anti-communism, with the veils to understanding only darkened by the Korean War, this approach became so entrenched that even as late as the mid-1960s, the hapless political science major who searched for a syllabus that included China, would most likely have found it only in a course entitled "Totalitarian Systems."

The fateful mid-1960s, however, were at last to change this. Two quite disparate sets of factors were influential in the gradual move away from the totalitarian paradigm in China studies. First was the *coincidental* emergence of late-Maoist political philosophy on the one hand and of a robust younger generation of American China scholars on the other, men and women who were deeply affected by the war in Vietnam and troubled by its many parallels with earlier Chinese (and American) experiences. As for Mao Thought, stressing as it did class struggle and contradiction even under socialism, it patently played a major role in precipitating the violent social and political wrenchings of the Cultural Revolution. And as that painfully revealing drama was unfolding inside China, most younger China-scholars-in-the-making on the outside were finding in the Vietnam war and the means of its waging ample cause to reject old orthodoxies about both communism and Asia. As they observed the courage, the suffering, and the treacherous politics on all sides of the struggle for a national socialist revolution in Vietnam, and simultaneously watched the many-colored, fine-embroidered fabric of China's own socialist polity ripped and unraveling before their eyes in the unprecedented storms of the Cultural Revolution, such stark and oversimple formulations of the dynamics of communist systems as were laid down in the totalitarian model were bound to fall into scholarly disuse. Throughout the late 1960s and early 1970s, Mao and the other high party/state leaders, far from radiating totally penetrating power and exerting total control, seemed to lurch from crisis to crisis trying to contain or to redirect the various forces (from within the state itself and from without) that sought to challenge and erode even the semblance of unified authority in China. Sometimes, it became clear, the party/state was barely able to hang onto the reins of control. Even after the most volatile of the Cultural Revolution storms had subsided, it remained apparent that the state under Mao, like the society it struggled to govern, was a highly complex composite of differentiated forces, not amenable to neat packaging in totalitarian terms.

The second set of factors shaking China studies loose from the totalitarian model derived from changes in the wider scholarly enterprise of political science in the 1960s. Biographical, historical, and institutional approaches to political explanation gave way before the battle cries of the "behavioral revolution." Studies of the state as such, and most other research conceived within a "state-typological" or "state-society" framework, lost their intellectual and professional appeal as the laurels of a newly self-conscious social science went to those who analyzed instead the various roles and behaviors of political "rational actors," along with their conditioning constraints. Since China at that time still remained resolutely closed to foreign social researchers interested in studying political behavior through participant observation, attitudinal measurement, or systematic data collection of any sort, those who hoped to apply the best of the new political science concepts and approaches to the Chinese case were effectively forced to confine their studies to those "political actors" whose movements and methods were at least dimly visible from vantage points outside the system—that is, to the supreme elite. With all the other realms of Chinese political life closed to scientific exploration, inquiring eyes were necessarily trained on those flickering images of Mao himself and that handful of his revolutionary comrades who inhabited the misty regions at the very top of China's political pyramid.

Naturally, the weight of these two separate sets of factors was to fall rather differently on different individual scholars. Some concentrated more on revising and enriching our understanding of socialism and the revolutionary process. Others focused on selecting and perfecting *realpolitik* models of regime policymaking. Though the line between the two was not a solid one and each clearly profited from the research and writing of the other, it may be only a small exaggeration to suggest that by the early 1970s the scholarly field of Chinese politics could have been divided roughly into two groups of researchers: those who thought of themselves primarily as students and interpreters of the Chinese "revolution," and those who regarded themselves chiefly as watchers and analysts of the Chinese Communist "regime." Neither group, as it turned out, made state-society relations a focus of their work.

Those whose subject was "the revolution" tended to study the party more than the state. Party ideology, especially Maoist ideology, party behavioral norms, the party's "mass line" workstyle, and party propaganda techniques and political models were all carefully analyzed for what they could reveal about the essence of the revolutionary process. The transformation of values Mao was determined to bring about, the relation between socialist ends and revolutionary means, the contrasts with Leninist and Stalinist principles of organization and practice—all these were well depicted in learned and sensitive studies of socialist China's new patterns of political participation, party rectification, and mass socialization.[2]

If there was a theory of state-society relations implicit in some of these studies, it was perhaps that the Chinese Communist Party had taken on the role of society's agent within the revolutionary state.[3] But when they did offer a general analysis of Chinese social organization, these studies frequently followed too closely the main lines of official "class analysis" propounded in Beijing. In the absence of independently confirming empirical sociological research—and without the feel that such research would have given us for the size of the gulf (inevitable in all systems) between political rhetoric and social reality—the nearness of fit between those official class categories and the actual forces defining and animating Chinese social life under Mao inevitably remained open to serious doubt. Thus, the genuine dynamics of state power and social change generally fell disappointingly outside the scope of these studies, even as they provided us with a sophisticated grounding in the discourse and ideals of Chinese politics.

Those scholars whose subject was "the regime" were meanwhile making no less a contribution. Their researches yielded quite a rich variety of conceptual frameworks or part-theories of the dynamics of Chinese elite politics. Although some of this work took the form of general, descriptive, institutional studies, still essentially concerned to chart the formal organization of Chinese party, state, and policymaking procedures,[4] other studies turned their focus on the informal behavioral norms of the career bureaucrat, the ethos of compromise and survival, and the unspoken rules of the game of Chinese elite politics.[5] A great many studies of policy and decisionmaking tended to take a Mao-centric or even a "Mao in command" approach.[6] Other scholars, however, found it useful to deploy a "generational" model of intra-elite differentiation and conflict.[7] A few others argued for a "factional" model as the key to unlocking the mysteries of high-level political struggle in Beijing.[8] These latter two sorts of models classified Chinese decisionmakers primarily according to accidents of their individual backgrounds and experiences that presumably conditioned their political goals and delimited their choices among potential political allies.

Still other researchers tried setting aside such personal networks and individual attributes and, borrowing from the "bureaucratic politics" model as it was used in the study of U.S. foreign policymaking,[9] sought to explain Chinese decisionmaking in terms of the organizational interests pursued by competing ministries, bureaus, and other agencies within the party/state apparatus.[10] Policy and policymaking gradually became the dominant subject matter of the literature as important studies appeared covering science and technology policy, national minorities policy, sent-down youth policy, industrial management policy, public health policy, agricultural mechanization policy, urban social organization policy, bureaucratic management policy, and commerce policy.[11] The focus on policy led many analysts implicitly or explicitly to favor "policy group" or "tendency"[12] models to explain particular struggles and outcomes. Scholars disagreed about how these groups of elite political actors should be delineated and about how the bundles of policy preferences that presumably held them together (and apart) should be characterized.[13] But many came to the conviction that alternative political and economic policy packages existed in the minds of at least some Chinese leaders and were repeatedly involved in elite disputes and compromises during the Mao years. Whether we were able to detect only "two lines" or three or more, it was established without much doubt that competing visions of the future of the Chinese polity were also at stake in the personal power struggles among the denizens of Zhongnanhai.[14]

If it could be fruitful to think in terms of organized bureaucratic interest groups and even policy groups contending inside the elite, it was only a short step to the hypothesis that interest groups and political opinion groups, based not in the party/state apparatus but in society itself, might also be contributing to the evolving political process in China.[15] A few provocative exploratory studies were also produced along these lines.[16]

This very profusion of analytical approaches may have helped lay to rest any lingering attachment to the totalitarian vision of the Chinese state as a monolith. The more case studies appeared, the more varied seemed the institutional and operational responses that could be employed within the system. The more we learned about the economy and how it was (and was not) regulated by the state, the more it seemed that much important authority had actually been decentralized or, as some preferred, "deconcentrated" throughout the system.[17] The more we studied policy formation and implementation, the more it seemed central leaders operated under many constraints, often failing to get their way; even more often, getting part of what they wanted but having, then, to cope with numerous unintended outcomes as well.[18] Clearly, the "great unity" pronounced periodically by propagandists in Beijing had been a very poor reflection, indeed, of the decision-making and administrative realities of life in China.

The cumulative teaching of twenty years of the best scholarly research on Chinese politics had patently driven us away from the image of a monolith and toward enormously contrasting conclusions and intuitions about what must have been the essence of life in the Chinese polity. Our studies had taught us that the state under Mao contained numerous shifting, cross-cutting, competitive (even hostile) centers of power. We had seen that the state almost never spoke to the people with one voice. We had learned that China's gargantuan and byzantine bureaucratic apparatus acted by no means as a mechanical transmission belt for central directives, but delayed, distorted, deflected and destroyed central intentions as often as it faithfully implemented them. We had determined that Chinese social life was by no means fully penetrated or effectively dominated by the revolutionary communist values of the party; that the perverse subculture of looking out for number one, of cultivating connections, of cheating the state and beating the system, was so widespread that it became pitifully difficult even for China's impressionable youth to secure their personal ideals in the official public philosophy. We had learned that state policy itself was often not the gloriously transformative, revolutionizing initiative it was heralded to be, but a series of forced compromises and squalid bargains— the best deals that could in fact be salvaged against the recurring hesitations of jumpy local officials and the surly resistance of entrenched political and economic interests. Our studies and analyses had made it clear that the very process of policy formulation was often a stumbling, fumbling affair, resting not on the eagle-eyed reconnaisance of an all-seeing state, but on wildly false information and conspiracies of misrepresentation pressed upward by the yea-saying apparatus. Our smorgasbord of approaches had yielded important insights.

Still, it remained unclear how so many partly conflicting part-theories about Chinese politics were to be reconciled. Some scholars implied that the best we might hope for was a deliberate sequencing and synthesis of the available approaches into a composite picture of the policy process. Thus, for example, we might finally conclude that in certain periods and on certain issues bureaucratic or factional politics were dominant, while in other periods or on other issues, intra-elite debate over policy content or interest group activity would prove most salient in explaining outcomes.[19]

Such deliberate eclecticism had its attractions, but it could only take us so far. It could not respond to the far greater problem or gap in theory that was urgently facing students of contemporary China: that of carving out an adequate approach to the study of state-society relations under Mao, and after Mao. All those part-theories of elite policymaking had helped undermine the totalitarian model, to be sure, but even when synthesized they were necessarily incapable of generating a real alternative to the totalitarian model for analyzing the basic relationships of China's state and society. For, with the exception of the "interest group" approach, which was not well-developed and which in any case did not appear to have a terribly promising future, none of the models of elite policymaking listed above even began to address the extent or nature of the interaction between state and society in Mao's China.

Assuredly, the assumptions underlying these policymaking studies may have worked well for conflicts *within* the state bureaucracy, where the quintessentially "pluralist" understanding of politics as a problem of allocation—"who gets what, when, and how?"—was clearly often the heart of the matter. But these approaches had little to teach us about the politics and the power of the state vis-à-vis society. Not only was the atomistic Western pluralist ethos of a healthy society as one spontaneously generating numerous diverse, competitive groups of individuals with self-defined, shared interests an ethos most alien to both tradition and contemporary social realities in China. This approach quite missed the point in a realm of other issues where the underlying understanding of politics is not as a problem of allocation but a problem of control, of rule, of us against them.[20]

One day, perhaps, pluralist assumptions about the nature of political competition may apply broadly to Chinese affairs. But for now, and ever since its inauguration in 1949, the Chinese party/state must be seen as a modernizing dictatorship, seizing resources from some segments of society to serve its planned goals of economic development and social transformation. This is not always *all* it has been, but as a self-described dictatorship (whether of the proletariat or of the vanguard) it has necessarily sought domination over certain elements in society. In seeking to dominate, it has provoked resistance; sometimes outright resistance, sometimes indirect or evasive resistance, and sometimes only privately internalized resistance, or alienation.

This reality of rule, of domination and resistance, is the larger context in which I believe our specialized studies of state, society, and politics in China ought now to be framed. The intra-elite struggles over allocations and over turf are importantly illustrative aspects of evolution in the polity that we must seek to capture and comprehend. But their true import can probably only be grasped by approaching them as fragments in a larger mosaic of state-society interactions, in which the state frequently seeks control and social forces often demur.

In the absence of such a conceptual framework, designed to assist us in studying the processes and the nodes of state-society interaction and integration, we were also necessarily without means systematically to explore those areas and cases where state organization and state ideals did *not* meet and did *not* successfully mesh with existing patterns of social organization or with popular culture(s). We were without a coherent approach to the evidence we saw of sporadic but widespread social resistance—that is, of popular rejection or evasion of various state policies, organizational forms, and procedures. We were also without a framework for investigating popular political heterodoxies and subcultures of resistance in the face of the party/state's attempts to enforce its own cultural hegemony.[21] Similarly, scholars were able to give but little sustained attention to those areas where (consciously or not) state policy had been molded by or otherwise adapted to abiding societal expectations and demands;[22] nor could there be very much written about the many ways in which the party/state's own organizations, methods, programs, and plans were, in fact, deeply imprinted by pre-existing and/or evolving forms of Chinese social organization and their attendant cultural norms.[23] The broad and deep interplay of impulses between state and society had not been adequately addressed either in the best interpretations of Mao Thought and party ideology or in our most painstaking analyses of power politics in Beijing.

It was not, of course, that the fundamentals of contemporary Chinese social organization and differentiation had gone completely unstudied. By the 1970s, able sociologists of a structuralist orientation were writing studies of mainland Chinese communities and groups that gave us an enhanced appreciation for the great variety of human experience under the regime of Mao. Indeed these studies were concerned precisely to display the disparity between the communal ideals of social organization articulated by the party/state and the real-life groups and subsystems—the villages, offices, workteams, and classrooms—in which the Chinese people actually made their lives. Portraying such people for the most part as rational, self-interest maximizers, these writers showed how some of the subsystems or structures they inhabited could be rather hospitable to the ideals of the party. Others they described were much less so. In fact, it seemed implied, one might think in terms of an array of social subsystems, some more and some less congruent with the ideals pronounced by the party.[24] Obviously, there were to be difficulties with an analytical approach that counterposed structures and ideals so sharply. The structures described in reasonably fine detail seemed to function so well at preserving and maximizing interests under the given conditions that it was difficult to see where any impetus for future change might originate. To quote from the concluding paragraph of one of the best of these studies, published in 1978:

Our analysis suggests that further marked changes in the character of village and family life can only come from further changes in the rural social structure, rather than from campaigns to combat old ideas and customs. Yet the current structure is a fairly effective one from the official point of view, and most structural changes would pose some threat to that effectiveness. Thus the current modus vivendi between the government and the peasants is likely to continue into the future, although gradual and incremental changes in the rural economy and health and educational situation can be expected to have some consequences.[25]

The problem with this passage is not just that from the vantage point of the late 1980s it seems to have been way off the mark as a prediction of the future. It is that making structure so central to the research effort imparted a certain stasis to the analysis, a certain inability to perceive the larger, protean process of history in which these structures were suspended, partly determining the process, to be sure, but partly determined by other elements suspended in the emulsion as well. E. P. Thompson has said that all structuralism ultimately amounts to is "*an exercise of closure* . . . a kind of intellectual agoraphobia, an anxiety before the uncertain and the unknown, a yearning for security within the cabin of the Absolute."[26] Whatever the truth of this general line of criticism, structuralism came to contemporary Chinese studies as a welcome ally in the effort to explode the totalist mythology. It left us, however, quite unprepared to foresee or explain the social realignments that were so quickly to come.

Now, perhaps, in the late 1980s, we are at last in a better position to provide more complex, more comprehensive, and more dynamic accounts of structural-cultural and state-societal relations in China. After all, the post-Mao relaxations and the policy of "opening" have given us considerably better access to the Chinese people themselves, across almost the entire country and in many different walks of life. And what these people are willing to tell us, while no doubt not completely candid, certainly seems on the surface to be much less constrained than before by political dogma and plain fear. Surely now we can hope that our work will take giant leaps forward in sensitivity and realism about both past and present.

Perhaps. But the scholarly tasks of reconstructing the social and political experience of the Maoist past in terms comprehensive, dynamic, and subtle enough to be genuine actually remain fraught with difficulty. For, from the very death of Mao and the arrest of the "Gang of Four," China's new leading coalition has been most diligently absorbed in revising the old Maoist conceptual framework for interpreting political events, and very busy reversing the official versions of China's recent social and political history. And thus, ironically, in the 1980s we can find some of the old myths of the monolith gliding effortlessly to the surface of discussion to becloud again the social science of contemporary China.

In Beijing, after the ouster of the ultra-left, the power coalition gingerly forming around the once and future chief, Deng Xiaoping, gradually consolidated its position. In the process, issuing what amounted to bulletins on its own health and success to the waiting people, the coalition offered official reevaluations of Mao, Mao Thought, and most of China's recent political history. The "cult of personality" was now no longer defended as an effective tool of popular mobilization, but deplored as an abomination of dictatorial ambition. The Cultural Revolution's colossal failure to safeguard intraparty democracy and the fundamental human rights of ordinary citizens was now blamed on excessive centralization of power and the residual bad habits of China's political culture—obsessive loyalism and mindless kowtowing to superiors in the hierarchy. The world was given to understand that the party/state, especially in Mao's final years, may ceaselessly have propagated an austere egalitarianism, yet actually had done little to promote genuine socialism. With all power amazingly concentrated in the hands of a very radical very few, it was possible somehow to browbeat and dupe much of the once revolutionary cadre corps into mercilessly disregarding the righteous demands of the people, chaining them instead to poverty and stifling their material and intellectual creativity. So history is abridged and adjusted to meet the needs of changing political conditions.

China's new leaders have provided for her people, and for the world, new official versions of the past and a new conceptual framework within which to explain the dilemmas and distortions of the Mao era: a framework featuring such constructions as "the cult of personality," "the ultra-left feudal dictatorship," and "the unlimited expansion and abuse of state power." Reformulations such as these, from 1976 on, have been widely welcomed both inside and outside China because they had the considerable virtue of creating some space for mutual forgiveness and renewed self-respect in a polity that had been rent by hateful accusations and personal moral degradation in Mao's declining years. If it could in truth be believed that the Gang of Four were not sincerely leftist revolutionaries but calculatingly evil tyrants, then most of those ordinary people who had fought for their sham ideals of "left socialism" could be legitimately reconceived as innocent dupes; and those who had opposed them could be vindicated.

After the purge of the ultra-left, China's new leaders did honestly face formidable tasks, and it would have been surprising indeed had they not felt the need to provide some such historical and theoretical space for social healing and the molding of a new and positive popular consensus on the good and bad aspects of the past. But the irony, for us and for the Chinese people, is that the new framework in which the Mao era has been frozen, for the present at least, is none other than that of totalitarianism! The irrational dictator, the super-penetration of the state into daily life, the passive capitulations of community and society, even the terroristic abuses of power by police and low-level functionaries and the virtual brainwashing of the people by means of continual ideological bombardment—all the elements of the totalitarian vision are there in the new leadership's critique and indictment of the past.

A few analysts in this country have already absorbed some of this vision and vocabulary into their retrospective accounts of Chinese affairs in the last two decades of Mao's leadership. (Solemnly we may read in such studies that Mao's China was not socialist after all, it was feudal. Or it was fascist. Or it was feudal *and* fascist.)[27] But most of us are well aware that there can be no return to such simplistic and monolithic images of the relations between state and society. It is most important that (at a minimum!) we hold onto our hard-won appreciation of the patterns of segmentation or structural differentiation within the state itself, and within society under Mao. (Indeed, there is much more work to be done in specifying these patterns and their consequences.) If Chinese leaders now have certain reasons to deploy, and the Chinese people certain reasons to accept, totalitarian imagery in explaining the past to each other, we at least must meet our obligation to continue questioning that simplistic imagery and to seek more subtle categories to convey all the complexities that we know were involved. This quest for more adequate approaches to state and society in the Mao period is, at bottom, what drives the three other experimental essays in this volume. Before turning to them, however, a few words should be said about the nature of the method they sometimes presuppose and sometimes seek to illustrate.

"Social Intertexture": *A Process Approach*

Given the scholarly distance that has been traveled, then, from the 1950s to the 1980s, what might now be proposed as a fruitful approach to learning about state, society, and politics in contemporary China? First, I believe, it is most important that we begin our work from the conscious knowledge that our overall analytic task is one of addressing not a mechanism, not a system, but *a process*; and nothing that we are able to learn about social structures and state structures should be allowed to obscure this consciousness of process. To regard ourselves as students of process will mean paying attention to history, of course, and sometimes even to individuals—to the effects, that is, of particular choices and unique events that might have happened otherwise. But the kind of process I have in mind is more than tracing mere sequence or searching for some sign of evolution *through time*. It is more than a narrative history of "shocks to" or "cumulative effects upon" the polity, where the polity is still portrayed as a more or less solid object. A politics-as-process orientation to our studies would, rather, lead us to explore for patterns of flux and flow among those *internal* elements, arrayed in tension, that constitute and animate the polity itself. In particular, such a process approach would press us into recognition of all those mutually conditioning interactions that occur among elements of the polity that we are accustomed to think of as rather distinct and often, therefore, as rather static.

To illustrate what I mean by a process approach, let us reconsider the two pairs of dichotomized analytics so often referred to in this essay: structure/culture and state/society. If we were accustomed to think of the Chinese polity as composed of elements of structure (institutions, organizations, routines . . .) on the one hand, and elements of culture (attitudes, beliefs, symbols . . .) on the other, then an internal process orientation might lead us to focus on those mutually conditioning interactions between the special elements of structure and culture in Chinese affairs that have yielded unusual power or unusual distress. Thus, the establishment of certain kinds of *institutions* in a social environment with certain prevailing *attitudes* may promote the development of certain new forms of *organization*, which in turn may undercut some formerly held *beliefs* and thus encourage de facto work *routines* not consistent with traditional *symbols* of the healthy polity . . . and so on. The oscillating interaction between elements of structure and elements of culture is the hallmark of this route to explanation. And as a guide to research and argument, it accords with the view, now quite general I believe, that the social structures we observe are at once reflections and determinants of a community's cultural codes and ideals.

So too with elements of state (bureaucracy, army, party . . .) and elements of society (elites, villages, families . . .), an explanation might well run that the creation of the postrevolutionary *bureaucracy* altered the previously available routes to *elite* social status, making an *army* career more desirable and thus heightening competition within the *village* for the privilege of enlisting, resulting in several members of the revolutionary *party* succumbing to illicit pressure and breaking party discipline by granting favorable treatment to certain *families* over others . . . and so on. To repeat, the steps in the argument turn on the mutually conditioning interactions between elements of state and elements of society. And again, the method accords with the general view that the forms and actions of states are at once the causes and the consequences of the forms and relations of the societies in which they arise.

It is on this continuous, mutually conditioning interplay between *unlike* elements that I want to insist. If this were our focus, our orientation to the study of the Chinese polity, then we might regard ourselves as analysts of the entire, intricate *social intertexture* that forms the stuff of political life. In fact, study with conscious reference to the elaborate social intertexture of political experience can serve as a handy label for the approach I advocate. But the term may require clarification.

"Social" here is used in its inclusive, not exclusive, sense. I do not mean "social" as opposed to economic, cultural, political, and so on. I mean it deliberately to include all those not-to-be-compartmentalized dimensions of the human experience that we normally study under the "social sciences": anthropology, economics, politics, sociology, and the best part of history.

As for "intertexture," the *Oxford English Dictionary* defines it as "The action of interweaving; the fact or condition of being interwoven." And the first two examples of proper usage for this noun come from J. Taylor (1649), "Like vowels pronunciable by the intertexture of consonants"; and from L. P. Johnson (commenting on Pope, 1779–81), "He always considered the intertexture of the machinery with the action, as his most successful exertion of the poetical art." These examples justify, I think, the choice of what may seem a neologism. They suggest that, unlike an ordinary weaving—a silk tapestry or a wool carpet—which we may expect to be made entirely out of threads of the same material differing only in hue, an intertexture can be accomplished with things of different sorts: with vowels and consonants, with machinery and action. In fact, the significance or the artistry of an intertexture seems to derive from the very interweaving of *unlike* elements into new compound wholes. Without both vowels and consonants, efforts at speech are unintelligible. Subtle sentiment may be expressed without the disciplined structure of verse, but we will call it mere prose. Trivia may be set to meter and rhyme, but we will regard it as doggerel. The "poetical art" is achieved only in the interweaving of these *un*like elements; form and content, structure and meaning. So too it is, and must be, I believe, in the art of the "science" of society. But, concretely now, what "methodology" would this notion of social intertexture imply? How shall we frame and execute our studies? How construct our arguments? To me it suggests struggling to keep a kind of deliberate double vision in all the work we do. We must train ourselves to see *at once* both the minutest of minor details and the most grandiose of grand designs. We must search, with magnifying lenses, deep in the fabric of the social intertexture for the winding paths taken by each and every filament; but also step back to appreciate the art and meaning of the overall pattern of the social tapestry. And since, practically speaking, actually to see both *at once* is probably not possible, we will have to proceed by performing a constant series of conscious juxtapositions of our perspective. This is not unlike the method of interpretive anthropology called for by Clifford Geertz, which requires "a continuous dialectical tacking between the most local of local detail and the most global of global structure in such a way as to bring them into simultaneous view."[28] This is not a method of study, argument, and explanation to end our reliance on dichotomous analytics such as structure/culture or state/society. At first, in fact, it may only seem to add yet another dichotomized dimension—that of detail/design—to the analytic baggage we haul with us into the field. But if an effort at continuous juxtaposition of viewpoints and continuous tacking between the small realities, understandings, or events and the large ones *were* consciously carried through, I believe the very effort itself would help discourage recurrent tendencies toward narrow, unidimensional, or static assumptions, and would push us instead toward more fluid conceptualizations of the interplay of forces that shape and reshape the polity. There may be no categories of experience we can invent comprehensive enough to encompass and compare what the osprey and the flounder "know" of the world. But we must try to comprehend something of each, and something of the fluid dynamics of air and water as well, if we are to understand what "really happens" in the dive. Ultimately then, moving from thread to pattern to thread is a methodology calculated to help us spot as many points of mutually conditioning interaction as we can, not only *along* each dichotomized analytic dimension we employ, but eventually, perhaps, even *across* them.

This is an ambitious course to recommend for the study of *any* contemporary polity; and for the study of China, where so much remains only half-apprehended, the recommendation may seem simply impetuous. For there is an obvious danger in such an approach, which would proceed through "an advancing spiral of general observations and specific remarks"[29] to an overall interpretation of structure and significance, action and meaning, necessity and potential, in the life of the polity. The danger is that if we are not very careful about our choice of categories and our treatment of evidence, our accounts may turn out to be not so much dialectical as merely circular. There is no simple solution that will dissolve away this danger, only the arduous one of practicing our craft with as much transparent integrity as we can summon, and with abiding modesty. The risk of idiosyncratic overinterpretation seems worth taking in the interest of bringing more of context, process, and interaction into our understanding of politics and the human condition in China.

Two

Peasant Localism and the Chinese State

A Center-Periphery Approach to the Evolution of State Socialism under Mao

All institutions acquire and seek some measure of autonomy, vis-à-vis the centers of power which would dominate them. Their autonomy consists in their unintegratedness into the order sought by the central authority of the society. EDWARD SHILS

*H*ow should we approach an analysis of the structure and roles of the Chinese state? How, in particular, should we formulate questions about the relations of state and society in China? About the linkages between units embedded in the structure of the state apparatus on the one hand, and units embedded in the evolving social structure on the other? Are all "state socialist" systems like China state-dominated ("statist") in the same ways and to the same degree? If not, what concepts should we be using to uncover salient differences and their causes?

Challenging and worthy as such questions about method and conceptual orientation may be, I would not necessarily raise them for their own sake. Unsettled curiosity about yet another broad question, however, seems to require that they be confronted. That question, stemming from revolutionary Marxism's greatest historical irony, is not the one so often posed about *why* communist parties came to power where they did, but one much less studied: *What difference* has it made, for subsequent political development under socialism, that the major socialist revolutions took place not in advanced capitalist socioeconomic formations under the leadership of alienated, politically conscious, and highly militant proletarians, but in societies that were overwhelmingly peasant, technologically not up to world standards, and suffering from conditions of extreme scarcity?

Noting this irony as a fact of twentieth-century revolutionary life has, of course, become commonplace. American social scientists often note it, with apparent glee, as definitive refutation of the Marx-Engels theory of historical development. European Marxist theorists tend to note it with a chagrined shrug, returning, it often seems, without missing a beat to their own analyses of contemporary *capitalist* state structures. Neither of these groups has yet contributed very much to our understanding of the structural or programmatic possibilities for socialist governments in states that, like China under Mao, are mostly peasant and very poor.

Available Approaches

Ever since the 1950s, students of contemporary China have been working their way through a number of evocative models of state power and social response that are relevant to these questions. The bleak and ultimately ahistorical "totalitarian" models, the excessively mechanistic "cyclical" theories, and the obscurantist and question-begging "cult of personality" argument about the essence of Chinese state power and the means of its exercise were each at first embraced but later gradually abandoned by scholars. Surveying the literature of the 1970s, we find two general approaches to analyzing the Maoist state that seemed to hold the field. One was informed by the development of modern liberal capitalist states and by the discipline of Western political sociology. The other, in the Marxist tradition, regarded the state apparatus as the instrument of dominant class rule but also (following Trotsky's critique of the Stalinist state formation) as the potential seat of corruption and final betrayal of the socialist revolution.

The first of these, eclectically incorporating elements of group theory, exchange theories of power, and models of organizational behavior, made the important assumption that the socialist state, like other modern states, is a plural entity. State power, even in a socialist dictatorship, is shared among contending groups. The effective exercise of state power depends in the long run on the construction of viable coalitions among these groups. And the only way to understand both the extent of state power vis-à-vis society in China and the constraints on that power is to understand how contending political groups may reinforce or thwart one another's ends. Analysts of this persuasion could be found using interest groups, factions, opinion groups, occupational groups, other social strata, or informal regional and bureaucratic networks as their primary units of analysis. And often they disagreed profoundly with one another about the way to define the important contending groups.[1] But they did all share the view that in China, political struggles involving forces within the state apparatus itself were the dominant determinants of the direction of state policy, and that the sum of state power in society would have to be understood in its parts.

In the other group were the writers who basically accepted the Marxist analysis of the functions of the state and were inclined to believe that under ideal conditions of worldwide prosperity and socialist revolution, states could indeed wither away. However, under real conditions of economic backwardness and extreme scarcity—such as in Russia in 1917 and in China in 1949—they believed the seizure of power by the Marxist party must necessarily be followed by the consolidation of strong state power, first to direct national economic development toward the point of abundance for all, and second to suppress counterrevolutionary class remnants and bourgeois tendencies that might poison the political and social atmosphere and obstruct the evolution of true socialist consciousness among the masses. The "dictatorship of the proletariat," exercised by the party/state apparatus on behalf of the working masses, had to be stern to safeguard the political and social gains of the revolution, while the economy, as it were, had time to catch up. The *problematic* in analyzing the socialist state was, for these writers, then, knowing the extent to which any given party/state apparatus strove to build socialism by socialist means, preserving a revolutionary, egalitarian political and social atmosphere that might permit the working masses gradually to take charge of their own affairs. Analysts in this tradition, who saw the socialist state as a singular tool of either proletarian or bourgeois class domination, did not have very much cheerful news to report. In 1936, Trotsky himself had written of the record of state socialist guardianship in the USSR:

The basis of bureaucratic rule is the poverty of society in objects of consumption, with the resulting struggle of each against all. . . . Such is the starting point of the power of the Soviet bureaucracy. . . . A raising of the material and cultural level ought, at first glance, to lessen the necessity of privileges, narrow the sphere of application of "bourgeois law," and thereby undermine the standing ground of its defenders, the bureaucracy. In reality the opposite thing has happened: the growth of the productive forces has been so far accompanied by an extreme development of all forms of inequality, privilege and advantage, and therewith of bureaucratism.[2]

It was a grim logic. Concessions inevitably had to be made to "bourgeois right" and to inequality in the distribution of desirable things. The socialist state bureaucracy had precisely the responsibility for making those unequal distributions and it naturally did not neglect itself. As Trotsky perceived, "it of course draws off the cream for its own use."[3] The bureaucracy, thus reinforcing as it went anti-socialist norms of hierarchy and privilege, "rises above the new society" and in effect usurps power, ceasing to be the mere tool of the workers' state and becoming instead its increasingly bourgeois and despotic master.

Thus, the key questions in this approach involved not primarily the interrelationships of various bureaucratically anchored groups within the plural state structure itself, but rather the political and economic relation of the bureaucracy as such to society as a whole. In the face of the inevitable corrupting temptations of the state socialist situation thus understood, everything often seemed to depend on the leadership's

maintenance of a strongly egalitarian revolutionary orientation in both long-range development strategy and everyday
political practice. The potential for a thermidorian reaction
under state socialism was thought to be so great that evaluations of the health of the revolution in any country gave primary weight to the relative development of a culture of "bureaucratism" and *embourgeoisement* among the apparatchiks
and the party cadres. Hence these approaches, although off-
shoots of a materialist analytic tradition, often gave nearly
exclusive attention to levels of political consciousness, to
political-cultural and other "superstructural" elements of a
given society's development.

And on these dimensions, Mao's China tended to earn very
high marks indeed. A highly egalitarian orientation characterized the Chinese Communist Party's general economic development strategy and its distribution policies and methods
under Mao.[4] A plain, even austere, proletarianism was then
the hallmark of Chinese political culture. And that austerity
was widely thought to be the chief Chinese contribution to
Marxism-Leninism and more particularly the contribution of
Mao Zedong's dominating influence on the course of political
struggle in China after 1949. His personal intolerance of all
forms of bureaucratism and his tendency to stress the potential triumph of militant willpower over seeming material necessity were usually given much of the credit for what analysts
of this school regarded as China's tougher-than-average resistance to the hierarchic, statist, and bourgeois plagues that in-
fest state socialist systems.[5]

So strongly did some writers in this tradition believe that
the very nature of the state in China depended on Mao and a
handful of other top leaders in Beijing, that when Mao finally
died and his four leading leftist followers were purged, these
theorists perceived the result to be an immediate qualitative
change for the worse in the relation of the state to society in
China.[6] It was not necessary to wait and see how much and in
what ways the previous development strategy would be al-

tered by the new leadership; not necessary to see if residual Maoist methods and beliefs at lower levels of the bureaucracy might serve to block or modify centrally mandated policy changes; not necessary even to see how the working masses of Chinese would react. Since the all-important political tone-setting function was thought to rest at the very apex of the elite, these theorists needed only to evaluate the beliefs and actions of a few men in Beijing to know the historic course and nature of the Chinese state. After all, had they not witnessed the bourgeois revisionist ossification of enough other socialist dreams to know when they saw it coming?

This approach to the state ultimately focused attention, then, on the character of the supreme political elite of China. This was a focus it shared with the "plural state" approach, for although the plural state analysts did have room in their models for the actions and reactions of grassroots constituencies, they rarely actually mentioned them and seldom included "the masses"—working people not in the bureaucracy—in their analyses. In discussing "local" groups and forces, they did not usually dip below the level of bureaucrats working in the provinces and the largest municipalities.[7] This in itself could be interesting, of course. But the even more challenging and complex articulation of the relationship between the segmented bureaucracy they saw and the segmented society over which it operated was generally no part of their analysis. The lacunae these two approaches left in our understanding of state-society relations in China seemed especially great and troubling when the subject under discussion was the administration of rural or "peasant" China. For such an inquiry into patterns of action and belief and the nature of power relations very far from the political center, it clearly seems we need another analytical orientation.

Before moving on to that, however, I would emphasize that it is not necessary to reject outright either of the two approaches just described. Each has already made important contributions and continues to be capable of shedding much light on China's state and politics. Most students of Chinese affairs today automatically combine elements of both approaches in thinking about problems of political development. I do believe, however, that it is important to appreciate these approaches for what they have been—tools for analyzing *elite* political activity and the upper-level policy process, not for understanding the deeper structures and processes of state administration or the evolving relationships between state structures and underlying social organization. These are the matters that occupy the remainder of this essay.

A Center-Periphery Approach

To answer those first questions about the broad range of state-society relations in Mao's China, then, what we need is an approach that will direct our eyes not to forms of coherence and cleavage solely at the very top of the political pyramid, but to patterns of cleavage and integration throughout the entire society and polity. What we require, in other words, is an approach that will facilitate consideration of (1) the extent of social integration achieved and not achieved in China under Mao; (2) the patterns of social-structural division that remained or were intensified during that period; and (3) the relations of the forms and activities of the developing state apparatus to each of these. The existing center-periphery models of social organization, although they come with a variety of intellectual pedigrees and special emphases, can provide a valuable starting point for such an inquiry.[8]

Center-periphery theories tend to begin from two important general observations: first, that complex societies all have a center or core area; and second, that the center has a tendency to expand. The center of a national (or transnational) social system can usually be located spatially, but location is not its primary attribute. The center is defined, rather, as having a high concentration of the main elements of authority and power in the social system. The center is the social zone where authority is possessed; the hinterland or the periphery is the social zone over which authority is exercised. And, as Edward Shils has said, "Authority has an expansive tendency. It has a tendency to expand the order which it represents toward the saturation of territorial space."[9] As central authority successfully expands toward the periphery, the end *result* is greater *social integration*.

Different center-periphery theorists emphasize different aspects of central authority, and thus different dimensions of the process of social integration attendant on the expansion of central authority. Functional sociologists, like Shils, stress the normative aspects of central authority and thus the weakening of primordial values and loyalties as central authority reaches toward the periphery. Organizational-behavior theorists stress the bureaucratic-administrative aspects of central authority and thus the greater regulation and rationalization of the social system as central power extends toward the periphery. World-systems political economists and theorists of "internal colonialism" stress the economic aspects of the center's power and thus the deepening economic exploitation, immiseration, and dependency of the periphery that accompany central expansion. These different emphases lead in turn to different depictions of the groups operating at the periphery. They may be regarded as benighted parochials resisting incorporation into the "great tradition" value system and not fully participating in the national political system. They may be regarded as extralegal, corrupt, and anti-social pockets or enclaves defying regulation for the larger social good. Or they may be seen as the exploited, defenseless victims of central elites who use their power primarily to promote their own economic interests in ways that keep the periphery poor, underdeveloped, and dependent.[10]

Most of these theorists are not generally guilty, as is sometimes charged, of taking a truly unidimensional approach to problems of social integration. Close reading usually reveals their awareness of and sensitivity to other facets of the complex processes they seek to explain. But in choosing to emphasize just one of these broad dimensions of social coherence—political/administrative, economic, or normative/cultural—they inevitably provide a partial picture and one that colors their evaluations of the claims of center and periphery against each other. If we are to avoid this pitfall as we apply the concepts of center, periphery, and social integration to the Chinese case, we must make room in our analysis for all three of the broad dimensions listed above. In later sections of this essay, therefore, I will sketch the ways one might pursue an argument about social integration in Mao's China along each of these dimensions. First, however, we must try to purge some surrounding confusions about the nature of state "center" and rural "periphery" in the Chinese case.

Types of State Center

Because center-periphery theorists accept the notion that the center of society has a tendency to expand, it is often supposed that they hold that greater and greater levels of social integration will be achieved in the course of human history. Especially when a center-periphery approach is linked with "modernization" theory, there appears to be an underlying assumption that ever more social integration and ever-greater central penetration of the periphery of society is the natural and inevitable outcome of human development. Perhaps this is to caricature the work of the theorists in question. For even Shils, who is probably most vulnerable to a critique of this sort, has shown acute awareness of the unevenness of the "progress" of social integration over time. Partial integration often generates resistance to further integration, he says; and tighter integration in one area of social life need not imply that other areas will follow suit:

Integration is . . . not an indefinitely extensible condition of society. Human beings have limited capacities for integration, and the collectivities they form likewise have limited capacities. The increase in the integra-

tion of society occurs at the expense of the internal integration of parts of the society and some of the most important limits to the integration of society are thrown up by the exertions of the communities, corporate bodies, and social strata to maintain an internal integrity which would be lost by a fuller integration into society.
Integration is an intermittent phenomenon. Sometimes it is high in the relations of one sector of society to the center, at other times it might be suspended or loosened; at still other times in the same sector and within a relatively limited time period, integration might be modified into some degree of conflict, with some measure of integration persisting in that as well as in other spheres. Similarly, between points of time, parts of society which have been relatively closely integrated to the center can cease to be so, while others which have been relatively unintegrated might become more integrated. And then they might revert to the prior situation, but there is no inevitability in this.[11]

Still, basic notions of evolving social integration and a naturally expanding central authority do seem to mesh well with historical typologies of states that posit the ever-increasing size and functions of the apparatus over time, the ever-deeper penetration of state authority as human technological invention and economic organization become more complex, and the exceedingly "statist" character of what we like to think of as humankind's most advanced social systems. Take, for example, one very influential such typology, put forward by Harumi Befu in the late 1960s.[12] Befu posits three broad types of state—primitive, classical, and modern—that are distinguishable both in terms of their goals vis-à-vis the village periphery and in terms of their relative degree of "political" (or structural) complexity. Primitive states or centralized chiefdoms exist, according to Befu, in societies where "cultural elaboration has not reached the level of civilization, that is, a level at which the political elites . . . are clearly demarcated from village populations." Such states may indeed be despotic, but since bureaucracy is barely developed, rulers and ruled are not separated by a noticeable gulf in social status, and since the actual activities of the state such as taxation, conscription, public works, and adjudication "tend to be minimal," the village population does not find the state's demands and intrusions "onerous."[13]

Alluding in passing to the imperial Chinese state as an example, Befu characterizes the second type—the classical state—as one embodying greater cultural differentiation between the ruling elites and the mass. "[The] 'great tradition' as a way of life of the rulers separates them from the peasants, who partake of, at best, a folk version of the high culture." The bureaucratic organization of the state becomes more elaborate and more extensive, and rulers pursue political goals that are not necessarily in accord with the interests of the village masses and may be perceived by them as onerous.

With regard to the peasant periphery, the classical state has two major objectives, which must generally be met if the rulers are to maintain themselves in power: economic exploitation of agriculture and the enforcement of law and order in the villages. Social norms under the classical state grant it greater authority than the state in primitive systems. The state has "the right" to intervene in village affairs at the periphery to ensure that its two chief objectives of rural order and a flow of resources from the periphery to the center are achieved without serious interruption. In fact, however, classical states are organizationally weak, and direct interventions in village affairs are rare. The state must cultivate and rely on the indigenous village power structures to carry out important state policy at the periphery. State center and village periphery are now in an inimical relationship over some of the state's most vital objectives, and so classical rulers husband their legitimate authority to intervene. Peasant communities, in turn, take advantage of the state's organizational weakness and consequent failure to exercise its full authority. In the final analysis, villages independently manage most of their own affairs.

The modern state is a different matter. Its goals of penetration, control, and development are far more ambitious than those of classical state centers. Resting on a powerful industrial technology that facilitates political organization, communication, and socialization, it penetrates the periphery far more effectively in "an effort to obliterate the divergence between the political goals of the state and those of the village" through a "gradual appropriation of the political power of the village." Peripheral village communities and other groups are "integrated" or "incorporated" into the larger polity. They lose the relative autonomy that had characterized their relation to the classical state. Village government becomes a mere agent of the centralized, depersonalized state authority; little significant discretionary decisionmaking power remains at the peasant periphery. Indeed, peasants themselves should gradually disappear. Becoming "politically conscious" and learning to "identify themselves with the goals of the state," they are effectively "depeasantized," i.e. metamorphosed into "farmers" who are citizens of the whole state, no longer just families of their valley.[14] And, the typology concludes, no modern states succeed better at the total penetration of the village periphery than do socialist states. Furthermore, Mao's China, among the socialist states, is the supreme example of statist intrusion. Befu writes, "the modern state of Communist China . . . controls practically every sphere of peasant life."[15]

Other writers may put the case somewhat differently, but linking a center-periphery/social integration approach with the basic notions of political development theory will generally yield a picture of the evolution of states very like this one. What, then, is wrong with this picture?

First, the totality of state control over every aspect of peasant life that the typology mandates for the modern state is not borne out by the best empirical studies of the patterns and tenor of village-state relations in China after the revolution. This issue will be taken up at some length below. Suffice it to say here that while a few "model villages" in China in the 1960s and 1970s may actually have had their internal affairs dominated by political pressures from the center, our current understanding of conditions in more typical rural communities is that they were often in a position to bargain with central authorities and were able to deflect or reduce certain central demands made against them; that there remained considerable local discretion in the handling of various community affairs; and that state-sponsored social programs and goals actually made far less deep and permanent an impact on the values that guided peasant family decisions than outsiders often supposed.[16]

Second, the general typology suggests that political authority in a given system has a certain finite quality where village-state relations are concerned. Power is discussed as if it moved in zero-sum exchanges between village and state center: what the state gains the village loses, and vice versa. Befu writes, "We may contrast the classical state with the modern state by saying that in the classical state the village claims the power that legitimately belongs to the state, whereas in the modern state the state claims the power that traditionally has belonged to the village." Or again, "In the modern state, the central government exercises more and more power in wider and wider areas of village life. *As a consequence*, the area in which village leaders wield genuinely independent power gradually shrinks."[17]

But, as many theorists of different persuasions have noted, the sum of legitimate authority available within a social system is not fixed in this way.[18] In the evolution of most societies there are periods both of decline and of growth in the total legitimate authority commanded by central rulers and local leaders alike. The very capacity for authoritative political action within a given system is prone to vary, with other social conditions, over time. Certainly in the first half of this century, for example, the Chinese polity experienced a devastating net loss of legitimate political authority both at the center and at the periphery. At least for a time after 1949, by contrast, the sum of available political authority within the Chinese system was increased, and both central government officials and local community leaders shared in the new power.[19] Indeed, a convincing case can also be made that in the early 1950s, just as the new revolutionary government was extending its bureaucratic control deeper into the rural periphery than ever before in Chinese history, certain aspects of intra-village social differentiation were reduced in salience, through the social homogenization attendant on land reform and collectivization, making the identification of individuals with their own *locality* all the more important for political action and special pleading within the system.[20] Thus, as the center gained in power to command, *localities gained, too*, in power to implement or to resist.

At any rate, there is definitely reason to doubt that the balance of power between state center and village periphery is ever so violently tipped to one side as this typology's abstract ideal of the modern state suggests. How far and how violently the balance is tipped in a given polity probably depends heavily on which social groups are acting at the periphery, what specific administrative and other policies are pursued by the center to broaden or diminish the sphere of local authority, and how well those policies are implemented, evaded, or modified from unit to unit at the periphery.

This point is closely related to a third serious problem with a typology of states like Befu's: its lack of any well-delineated analysis of politically salient units and groups at the periphery. The deficiency is most glaring in the model of the modern state—and *a fortiori* in the modern socialist state—where it is assumed that the village world disappeared with the advance of industrialization, and that the distance between center and periphery has nearly vanished as high technology makes possible a level of mass political socialization undreamt of by even the most ambitious premodern rulers. The vision here is that of "mass society"—socialist or capitalist—in which parochial peasantries and other social groups that coalesce around primordial loyalties are replaced by white collar and blue collar citizens of the state, whose daily lives and work are quite fully integrated into nationwide political-administrative and economic networks.[21] The inadequacies of such a construct are well known even for the world's most industrially and technologically advanced societies. The protests and separatist demands of a host of localist, ethnic, religious, linguistic, and other primordial groups still bedevil the politics of such highly industrialized states as Great Britain, Canada, and the USSR. What, then, can we expect of such a model of state-society relations in a place like Mao's China, where the peasantry had most certainly not vanished, where industrialization had not proceeded very far, and where rapid communications, high-technology solutions, and national electronic media as vehicles of mass political socialization were but the daydreams of municipal planners who rode bicycles to work in offices where ceiling fans rotated languidly overhead and accounts were totted up on an abacus?

Although it had a socialist, modernizing elite and many of the aspects of a modern bureaucracy, Mao's China did not fit comfortably into the typology's slot for the modern state. Widespread rural illiteracy, technological backwardness, bureaucratic inefficiency and incompetence of alarming proportions, along with the confusions of chronic factional struggle at the party/state center—they all contributed to making the realities of Chinese politics in the 1960s and 1970s fall far short of what we should expect of the quintessential exemplar of modern totalitarian statist interventionism. First and most important, the peasantry (and "peasantness") as the foundation of the Chinese social formation had by no means disappeared.[22] Peasant communities may in fact have gained in self-consciousness, solidarity, and strength under Maoist policies. And the great unbridged gap between rural and urban living standards and life chances remained the painfully obvious primary dimension of Chinese social stratification throughout the Mao era.[23]

To respond within the terms of simple classification systems such as Befu's, then, the best we could do would be to say that

Chinese socioeconomy of the late Mao era was a composite of modern and non-modern elements. China, thirty years after the revolution, was still a society with an administratively well-developed socialist modernizing state center on the one hand, but a vast, backward, and ecologically very varied peasant village periphery on the other. But this would be to explain little while raising new questions about the depth of the peasant periphery and its real significance in the political mix. To move away from the limitations of ideal typologies and approach an understanding of the real range and patterns in the articulation of state-society relations in such a composite formation, then, we will have to look more seriously and critically at the structure of the periphery. We will have to delineate the nature of the basic units and forces operating there. We will have to confront China's fundamental "peasantness" and analyze its implications for the prevailing patterns of politics in order to grasp the true dilemmas of governance faced by her state socialist ruling elite.

Peasant Periphery

Much was altered in the countryside after the revolution. With Communist Party recruitment in the villages, mass mobilization efforts, and the establishment of functioning and credible local governments, the social distance between state center and village periphery tangibly diminished. Land reform followed by universal collectivization of agriculture made important changes in the traditional peasant economy, especially where property ownership and distribution of the means of production were concerned. Certain social policies, such as the pursuit of equal rights for women, also modified distinctive aspects of traditional life in rural China. Nevertheless, significant as these changes were, they fell far short of a thorough transformation of agricultural work or of village society. Chinese peasants were not turned into a rural proletarian class, earning set wages and working within the framework of a sharp division of labor. Farmers' incomes remained subject to the vicissitudes of the crop, and although most commodities markets were regulated by the state, small price fluctuations still could make a deep impact on peasant welfare in many areas. Rain or drought, insects or hail, the illness of a father, the birth of only female children—these and other determinants like them remained as central to the livelihood of Chinese peasant families under Mao as before. And despite the redistribution of wealth and the successive reorganizations of work units that came in the 1950s and early 1960s, the family household remained, as it was in traditional times, the primary social and economic unit in the countryside.[24]

The agrarian Chinese periphery continued to be made up of peasant families, hamlets, and villages. Those, in turn, were grouped around market towns, and as Skinner's important research demonstrated, successful consolidation of the large people's communes as viable economic and administrative units depended on including within their boundaries just the familiar villages of the peasants' presocialist standard marketing areas.[25] Since the population over most of rural China rose sharply over the three decades following the revolution, peasants may have come to have easy contact with more individual others than before. But for the great majority of rural-dwelling Chinese throughout the Mao period, all the meaningful social relationships of a lifetime would still be with other men and women *inside* these highly localized social units—the village and the commune. Marriage partners, in particular, would be sought from within the home commune and immediately contiguous ones. With opportunities for residential and occupational mobility close to zero for Chinese rural dwellers after the Great Leap Forward, the welfare of every individual must increasingly have come to be regarded as permanently tied to the welfare of that person's village or commune.

This is an important fact. It underscores that Chinese peasants, even as late as the decade of the 1970s, remained as

Skinner described them for traditional times, members of two small and overlapping local communities: first the hamlet or village, and second the marketing system to which their village belonged.[26] Those local marketing systems, roughly coextensive with the boundaries of the people's communes, remained, in turn, grouped around larger market towns that often served as the administrative seats of China's 2,000+ counties (*xian*). If, during the late Mao period, we had wanted to make a graphic representation of what Skinner has called "the basic ground plan of Chinese society," we would still have drawn a cellular formation, with individual units linked together to resemble a honeycomb pattern. The boundaries of those individual social cells were certainly not totally impermeable; but they were quite distinct. Insiders and outsiders were easily identified. Insiders were those whose life chances were determined overwhelmingly by factors internal to the local unit and whose aspirations, in normal times, could not reasonably extend far beyond its boundaries.

During the decade of the 1970s, peasant village and marketing communities produced and traded to serve internal consumption needs to a relatively high degree of *economic* self-sufficiency. And as for their internal *social* organization, it might, without wild distortion, have been regarded by some sociologists as attaining an even more perfect self-sufficiency. Following what Leon Mayhew has called a population-based approach to delineating the boundaries of a society, for example, it may well be that two or three adjacent marketing areas in the Chinese countryside during that period could have been analyzed as small societies unto themselves, operating relatively autonomously within the encapsulating larger society. Mayhew explains:

A society is sustained by a population. To establish the boundaries of a societal population we may adopt a definition of population quite similar to the one employed by bioecologists: A population consists of the self-perpetuating inhabitants of a territorial area. In this context the term "self-perpetuation" implies mating, and the term "inhabitant" implies relatively permanent residence. Thus, the boundaries of a population that sustains a society are established by the limits of the largest territorial area within which mating is common and residence is relatively permanent.

To start with the concept of population is not to define a society as consisting in its population. The society is not the population but the complex systems of action in which the units of the population participate.[27]

By this approach, since the cellular units of the Chinese peasant periphery largely satisfied the mating and residence requirements for demarcating societal boundaries, and since they also possessed coherent and relatively comprehensive cultural, economic, and authority networks—the chief integrating "complex systems of action in which the . . . population participate[s]"—these peasant communities could be analyzed as small but complete societies. This is a serious alternative to an approach to the peasantry formulated by Alfred Kroeber and Robert Redfield, which regards the peasant community as merely "a part society, with part culture," i.e. a subunit of the larger whole, which can be understood only by analyzing what it absorbs and what it rejects of the surrounding society.[28] Hamza Alavi, in a valuable article that touched on the problem of the encapsulation of peasant societies, rejected the notion of peasant communities as "small but complete societies." Alavi emphasized instead the profoundly penetrating impact of the surrounding society on the internal organization of peasant communities:

Indeed, the very structure of internal aspects of peasant societies is contingent on their relationship with the larger entity, insofar as the encapsulating state legitimizes and enforces property relations on which their internal differentiation is based. It establishes a whole paraphernalia of "law and order" which regulates transactions in property and commodities and impinges on a range of relationships between individuals and groups within peasant societies and those of the outside world.[29]

The combat of concepts at stake here has serious implications for evaluating the sustained cellularity of the Chinese periphery under Mao. To choose appropriate concepts and to begin to answer questions about complex social relations within Chinese peasant communities and between those communities and the outside world will require social science fieldwork of a sort that has only recently become thinkable for Western scholars.

Given the extreme diversity of conditions in the Chinese countryside, and the current relatively rapid rate of change under the post-Mao reforms, it will take many projects and many years before reasonable generalizations concerning these complex issues can be generated. Thus, in drawing attention to the cellular structure of the periphery in the decades following the revolution, we should certainly not rush to a premature conclusion that Chinese peasant communities were in their essence "small and complete societies," mostly "closed" to outside forces.[30]

The evidence of cellularity in the social organization of the periphery leads us only to two other complex sets of questions. First, if the cellular structure of society did indeed continue to prevail in the Chinese countryside, then one of the most important hallmarks of traditional peasant social formations survived thirty years of "socialist transformation" and rule by the Communist Party. This cellularity, or "vertical segmentation," is usually seen by theorists of peasant sociology to be so essential to the traditional peasant social formation as to be part of its definition.[31] If this key aspect of peasant society was preserved and perhaps strengthened under Mao, then it is reasonable to hypothesize that despite changes in the traditional agrarian property system, other important aspects of Chinese peasant culture, economy, and political behavior survived as well.

Second, if the Chinese periphery remained heavily marked by the structure of traditional peasant social formations, why was this so? It was not only Western modernization theorists like Befu, after all, who would have predicted quite a different peripheral social structure after thirty years of socialism. It was Lenin who spoke in 1919 of "abolish[ing] the difference between factory worker and peasant to make *workers of all of them*"; and who in 1920 saw the task of socialist development to require "abolishing the division between town and country, and making it possible to conquer completely and decisively the backwardness of the countryside, its scattered economy and its ignorance, from which stem all the stagnation, all the backwardness, all the oppression that have existed up to now."[32]

As China's socialist state center extended its authority over the periphery after 1949, it naturally made certain far-reaching changes in the structure of peasant society, but it may in some respects have preserved and strengthened the old peasant social formation as well. Did the Chinese Communists reject in their policies, then, the Leninist hope of making workers out of the peasantry? Or were they simply frustrated by the enormous, crushing inertia of their peasant periphery? Or did they find in the parochialism—the primordial peasant "localism"—that infuses a cellular social structure a force that could be made to coincide with and even reinforce the goals of socialist development?

In the sections that follow, we return to the problem of center-periphery integration in China and examine it along each of the three dimensions of social integration specified earlier—political/administrative, economic, and normative/cultural. In all three cases the evidence adduced is highly incomplete, the argument presented is only a sketch, and the object is merely to indicate what *types* of issues and questions would need to be considered to construct a balanced and compelling analysis of Chinese state-village (or center-periphery) relations. The thrust of the positions outlined, however, is twofold: (1) that the Maoist state gave clear central support for certain policies and institutional arrangements that had the effect of strengthening the solidarity and the interests of peasant communities against outside ("statist") domination;

and (2) that a full analysis might well reveal less direct and unmediated central penetration of the village periphery under Mao than is frequently supposed given our common assumptions about and models of "modern" state socialism.

Political/Administrative Integration

Most observers of Chinese affairs have concluded that the integration of center and periphery by the institutions of the political/administrative system was impressively thorough during the Mao years. An elaborate and resilient network of party and state cadres, who shared a single political vocabulary, stretched from the capital through each of the province centers and out even to the most remote mountain and grassland settlements. There is no doubt that the creation of a unified party/state structure penetrating to the grassroots was a first priority and one of the major early accomplishments of China's revolutionary rulers. Yet, no sooner was a tight vertical control network of ministries and bureaus set in place in the mid-1950s than debates arose within the elite about the overconcentration of power, and the search was on for effective means to *decentralize* some decisionmaking and coordinating authority to lower levels and units. How to prevent the rigid, vertically linked ministerial bureaucracies from pressing real power ever toward the top? How to consolidate procedures and institutions nearer the periphery to serve as counterweights to a distant and possibly misinformed or even misguided central authority? These were continually recurring themes in Chinese political debate, and they yielded some breathtakingly ambitious bureaucratic reforms, swift retrenchments, and further tinkering.

In his impressively conceived analysis written on the eve of the Cultural Revolution, Franz Schurmann explained the two forms of decentralization the Chinese leadership debated in the 1950s: decentralization of authority all the way down to individual production units, and decentralization only as far as regional party/state administrative offices.[33] In the late 1950s, despite the lack of a genuine consensus among the elite, the Chinese carried out what the Soviets, for example, had not been able to achieve—a major, across-the-board transfer of power from the central state ministries to the regions and especially to the provinces. But with the serious, sometimes desperate, economic reverses of the Great Leap Forward, which coincided with this experiment in decentralization, proponents of a reconcentration of power at the center and proponents of Libermanist decentralization to the level of the production units coalesced to regain the upper hand in policymaking. And by the mid-1960s, with the "little freedoms" concessions to agricultural production teams and the granting of "independent operational autonomy" to factory managers, the Chinese system of governance, planning, and administration had evolved into a curious amalgam in which decisionmaking authority was shared by center, region, and production unit.[34]

From the Great Leap's collapse onward, the chief characteristic of Chinese administrative organization was its apparently deliberate institutionalization of a certain tension between central and regional authority—that is, between the vertically linked state ministries and the regionally or horizontally based local planning committees. On Schurmann's interpretation, greater horizontal or regional authority meant power to the Communist Party, while greater vertical or ministerial authority meant power to state bureaucrats and technocrats. He saw the tension as one largely between "reds" and "experts."

Even at the time Schurmann was writing, this was probably the most doubtful aspect of his analysis. And since then, with continuing political upheaval and the revelations during and since the Cultural Revolution, it has become increasingly clear that horizontal or regional authority could not be equated either with political radicalism or with the representation of party interests as against state interests. The drama and struggle of the Cultural Revolution revealed that party cadres and state cadres usually understood their interests to be fully intertwined and often inseparable. Furthermore, "leftists" and "ultra-leftists" emerged from various points within the system, but tended to adopt their radical stances for personal reasons having more to do with their own class backgrounds and networks of friends, patrons, and associates than with their attachment to either horizontally regarding or vertically linked units of the bureaucracy.

What, then, was the nature and significance of the "tension" that was institutionalized in the interlocking structure of vertical and horizontal units? And how should we have regarded the probable political attitudes and loyalties of individuals serving within those linked but different offices and pathways of power within the system? Here, the cellular structure of the rural periphery that was being administered, the heightened community solidarity and peasant localism that infused that structure, and the related phenomenon of cadre "departmentalism" may afford us some clues. It seems quite clear that local cadres in horizontally regarding or regional units who stayed in their positions for any length of time inevitably came to identify with and represent the interests of their localities and regions. Their own careers and reputations were, after all, intimately tied to the fates of those areas and regions. The mindset of these local officials was strongly characterized by an inclination to pursue the interests of their own areas against other areas and, when necessary, against the demands of the vertical state apparatus.

What is most interesting, from the point of view of the other issues raised in this essay, is that horizontally based and vertically linked offices and authorities met and contended with each other at each tier of state administration moving outward from the center toward counties and even communes at the periphery. Thus, while the apparatus was undeniably highly integrated, the arrangement was one in which the interests of the increasingly segmented society and economy of the periphery were represented through a series of nested horizontal offices and committees that intersected the vertical lines of ministerial authority designed to link center and periphery. Now within this administrative gridwork, not all cadres in locality-based offices could pursue local interests with equal skill or enthusiasm; and some cadres in vertically linked bureaus may also have stood to advance their own careers by promoting the interests and the performance levels of the locality in which they happened to be assigned. Thus, we can no more assume perfect competition between these overlapping sets of officials than we can assume perfect complicity and cooperation. The structural deconcentration of authority institutionalized in this kind of a system, however, certainly suggests the hypothesis that it functioned, at least some of the time, to protect a cellular rural periphery against direct central penetration and control.[35]

Beginning from the village level, the first administrative units a peasant encountered clearly fit the cellular, population-based structure of organization. Production teams, brigades, and people's communes were all comprehensive units of territorial administration charged with responsibility for all aspects of economic development and social life in their areas. Only up at the county level could we begin to find a fuller complement of vertically linked ministerial bureaus pursuing more specialized tasks. But this vertical penetration was checked by a variety of horizontally based county offices, not only reflecting the demands of the county's various constituent units and communities, but also striving to integrate the ministerial bureaus' activities into an acceptable and workable plan for the development of the county as a whole. This criss-crossed administrative pattern was replicated, continuing up the administrative system, at the prefectural and provincial levels.[36]

The local or region-based officials at each of those levels almost certainly adopted different demeanors toward their superiors and toward ministerial cadres depending on the issues at stake. On some matters they may have adopted, for their localities, the demeanor of entitled claimants on upper-level or ministerial resources. On other matters they may have acted more like lobbyists seeking special consideration for their localities. On still other questions, they may have preferred to keep vertically linked offices at arm's length and, quietly mobilizing needed resources internally, may have adopted the demeanor of self-reliant, omnicompetent entrepreneurs, planning and executing local projects independently.

Central state officials, for their part, must also have acted in several different functional modes in their interactions with regional and local representatives; and a change in the central functional mode was likely to affect the demeanor local cadres adopted. When, on a given set of issues, for example, the state center was in its "beneficiary mode," emphasizing subsidies and redistribution of centrally controlled resources, locality-based officials at the periphery probably competed for central largesse, drawing attention to their area and emphasizing its accomplishments and its potential. If on a similar set of issues, the state center switched to its "extractive mode," emphasizing collections and tightening demands, locality-based officials probably scrambled for a low profile and sought protective complicity with ministerial cadres assigned to their areas. When the state center adopted a "routine managerial mode" on these issues, local cadres were likely to be inward-looking and absorbed by the special problems of their areas. But they may also, at such times, have articulated within the system their most accurate, or most truthful, perceptions of local realities.

With future research and refinements of simple hypothetical typologies like these, it may eventually be possible to develop an interactive model of the relations between state center and local cadres and of the administrative behavior of low-level officials and the variety of means they endeavored to employ to promote and protect the interests of their cellular social and economic units at the periphery. But one fact about their behavior is already clear from the very criss-crossed structure within which they worked: local leaders had to pursue a combined strategy of administrative activism *and* local political and economic entrepreneurship to serve their localities well. They had to work within the vertical administrative hierarchy, but also be able to mobilize a variety of horizontally based forces and controllers of needed resources. In a competitive system plagued by scarcities of all kinds, local cadres who did not operate skillfully within the criss-crossed administrative network would sooner or later disappoint their peasant constituents. This fact must have allowed them sincerely to justify many a parochial position and local protectionist stance or evasion in a morality of local solidarity that resonated well with the parochialism and localism of the peasants whose affairs they governed.

Economic Integration

State socialist systems, more or less by definition, seek to promote comprehensive and balanced national development through centralized direction of the economy. Conceiving of their task in terms of a worker-peasant alliance, central decisionmakers are supposed to plan a national network of exchange between industry and agriculture. The agricultural sector is to produce raw materials for industry and commodities to sustain the urban population; the industrial sector is to contribute agricultural producers' goods and consumers' goods to meet the peasantry's demands for an improved standard of living. But the state has a prior claim on the output of both sectors to promote the integrated development of the entire system. Thus Lenin could foresee a day when the parochial, self-sufficient, peasant family farms of the vast Russian countryside would be transformed under socialism into "meat and grain factories" producing specialized products for the state plan, with centrally allocated inputs and a division of labor similar to that prevailing in industry. The Soviet state-owned and managed machine tractor station network, to take one example, was intended as an important means of achieving industry-like planning integration and control over agricultural production. The ideal of rural work organization and rural economic development in China under Mao, however, was quite different. Although people's communes, brigades, and teams worked to targets derived in part from the state plan, they were generally not encouraged either to specialize or to depend on state-managed networks for major production inputs like tractors or irrigation equipment. In China, people's communes were not likened to factories but were regarded as multifunctional units for production, consumption, residence, social services, and development entrepreneurship. They were specifically urged to balance and diversify their local economies, producing a variety of crops and handicrafts, and even establishing light and heavy industrial installations *to meet their own needs* for energy, raw materials, machinery, and other inputs.[37] They were also specifically urged to be self-reliant in raising the capital needed to develop and expand their operations. State loans to agricultural communities were chronically scarce and therefore teams, brigades, and communes were expected to save out of their own surpluses, to investigate local market possibilities, and to make their own decisions whether to, say, set up a cigarette factory, a brewery, or a fruit-canning plant. Commune proposals for such new economic endeavors had to be cleared with county authorities to make sure they would not unduly compete for markets or resources with state-run enterprises. But the burden of development entrepreneurship and planning rested, in the Chinese countryside, not primarily with higher state officials, but with ordinary peasants, brigade and commune leaders who were expected to staff, finance, and incur the risks of new projects to generate income for the community.

The Bolshevik national "worker-peasant alliance" approach may well be regarded as having the disadvantage for a socialist polity of preserving two distinct classes and a considerable urban-rural gap in living standards and cultural amenities. It holds out the (very) long-term hope, of course, that with agricultural mechanization, more and more people will be moved off the land and into urban industrial jobs. They would, as Lenin said, be turned into workers, leaving machines behind them to do the drudgery and save them from the idiocy of rural life.

Chinese planners in the 1950s, '60s, and '70s, however, facing frightening demographic givens and with an initially very small and spatially concentrated industrial base, had a good deal less to say about the worker-peasant alliance and fought instead to keep people *on* the land. Their development strategy stressed labor-intensive farming to produce a greater agricultural surplus and locality-based economic development to generate higher rural incomes and enhance the availability of modest consumer goods, along with small-scale rural industrialization to provide a local supply of essential producers' goods. Chinese farmers, planning for their children's future, were not supposed to try to find them factory jobs in big urban centers, but to devise ways of industrializing and modernizing their own local economy to provide new jobs and a better quality of life in their own area.

While the development of China's strategic, high-technology, and major heavy and light industries was tightly planned and coordinated on a national scale, rural economic development was more loosely planned and coordinated on a local and regional basis. Certain key inputs serving agriculture, such as rubber and petroleum, did have to be allocated nationally through the state plan. Likewise, certain agricultural products, such as grains and edible oils, were tightly controlled. But much of the planning and investment for rural economic growth, and most of the supply and marketing networks serving rural communities, were coordinated at much lower regional and local offices. And considerable responsibility for generating entrepreneurial initiatives rested with commune members and local commune leaders themselves. As for county-level economic planning and coordination, by the mid-1970s it was often (if not, of course, always) conducted by local cadres with impressive vigor and comprehensiveness. Meanwhile, county and commune commerce administrators joined the locally bounded development effort and reinforced the segmentation of the rural economy in striving by all means to serve the major consumption needs of their population from within the boundaries of their own and nearby units.

In the political turbulence of those three decades under Mao, China's general economic development strategy underwent several permutations and some sharp reversals. It can also be argued, as Deng's followers now vociferously do, that on balance this rural development strategy was misguided and a failure. It neither adequately fueled the economy nor provided acceptable rates of growth and improvement in peasants' welfare. And as for Western economic analysts, different scholars have differently evaluated this peculiar pattern of locally coordinated investments and markets at China's rural periphery. Audrey Donnithorne, for example, called attention to possible redundancies, product quality losses, inefficient local market protectionism, and unrealized economies of scale that could impede real growth.[38] Others, however, cited factors like rural China's prevailing labor-to-capital ratios, its still poor national transport network, and the relatively widespread availability of coal as a cheap local energy source, and concluded that small-scale rural industries utilizing locally available resources and serving localized markets may have yielded faster and better-balanced growth in the medium term than could have been achieved by other means.[39]

The purpose here cannot be to try to settle these debates about the relative efficiency or inefficiency of China's small-scale autoindustrialization strategy. It is merely to indicate that such a strategy would and apparently did produce a pattern of integration quite divergent from the ideal type of centralized command economy associated with industrial socialism. The pyramidal lines of direct central intervention were cross-cut by the specific cellular plans and constraints in the honeycomb of units pursuing their localized economic development goals at the periphery. By encouraging the all-round agricultural, industrial, and commercial development of small county and commune units, the state center, on the one hand, enhanced the viability of locally bounded, internally integrated economic systems, and thus—at least in those localities where the strategy succeeded in promoting locally coordinated growth—established a kind of counterweight to centralized control. On the other hand, the state center evidently sought in this way to harness peasant localist and cadre departmentalist initiative to entrepreneurial tasks that coincided with its own national development goals.

While other modernizing state centers, socialist as well as capitalist, have seen in the vertical segmentation of their peasant peripheries signs only of the appalling poverty and backwardness that were to be swept away by the forces of modernization generated elsewhere in their economies, the Maoist state tended not only to tolerate peasant localism and cadre departmentalism, reinforcing the conditions under which they flourished, but also seemed to see in localist motives one of the more important mobilizable forces for balanced economic progress.

Normative Integration

The normative dimension of the integration of China's state center and its peasant village periphery is certainly the most difficult of the three dimensions to evaluate. For the most part, the aspects of traditional (read "backward") peasant culture the party/state wished to see disappear were clearly and consistently specified, as were the "progressive" norms and values it intended should replace them. Improvements over the years in mass media networks reaching into the countryside and effective use of other means of propaganda/education also ensured that the center's messages were, in some sense, getting through to peasants everywhere. The difficulty is in accurately gauging how deep the impact of centrally articulated social ideals actually was. How thoroughly were central norms internalized by rural people when they conflicted with traditional village norms? How successfully did peasants deflect the dissonant central ideals with which they were bombarded, or subsume them into the more familiar categories and concepts of local cultural patterns?[40]

True peasants, of course, are hardly ever "true believers." Not so tightly bound as we by the exclusionary logics of Western science and secular modern rationalism, peasants all over the globe tend to be unembarrassed eclectics in the terms they use to understand the natural world, and the most ecumenical syncretists in their absorption of various moral systems and traditions. Thus, on a question about the weather, peasants will generally see no good reason not to consult with both the meteorologists and the spirits. And on a question of local administration, a village head may choose a particular course of action as much because it fits with a folk-Confucian concept of upright behavior as because it is what the Communist Party and Chairman Mao might recommend. Certainly the rapid reflowering in the 1980s of traditional peasant religious and cultural practice must suggest that those older habits, customs, and beliefs remained a vigorous part of peasant consciousness all through the years when everyone was constrained to speak publicly in the terms of Maoist Marxism. It could hardly be clearer that the principles of Maoism, when *added* to the moral vocabulary of peasants, did not *drive out* other systems of meaning and concepts of value. Nor should it be regarded as a challenge to either the wisdom or the potency of any of the belief systems involved to note that they were capable of reasonably comfortable cohabitation in peasant minds. Urban groups of fragile and modern definition may slide softly into the thrall of a modern ideology. Peasants, in their segmented small communities, participate in a much more resilient, more anciently rooted, and many-layered counterculture. No matter how saturating the propaganda barrage, we should expect peasants to be the last group to fall before the singular logic and moral purism of scientific socialism.

Nevertheless, most observers would agree that the historically great gap in China between the high culture of the center and the folk culture of the periphery diminished somewhat in the years after 1949. Central social ideals and rural village values did seem to share more of the same conceptual ground then, and therefore, to show greater congruence than before the revolution. Most observers would also agree, however, that the major steps toward greater normative integration of center and periphery were taken not in the ideological propaganda drenchings of Mao's later years, but during the first national land reform and early collectivization efforts of the 1950s. Since those early days, movement toward greater normative integration appears to have been far more fitful and uncertain. In fact, some of the 1950s social-structural changes at the village level were so successfully consolidated that, ironically perhaps, they may themselves have stood in the way of subsequent central efforts to promote even more "advanced" socialist values and behavioral norms.

For example, the peasantry's adaptation to the early modest forms of collectivization may have served to strengthen and newly legitimize certain forms of particularism or localism that were already characteristic of traditional village life. The very process of administering land reform and collectivization, after all, did reaffirm the peasant family as the basic social and economic unit. And except for a brief challenge to some of the functions of the family during the Great Leap, the Chinese leadership consistently supported peasant family solidarity as the bedrock of the socialist social system. Furthermore, collectivization itself created additional new local solidarities, as the sociologist William Parish has pointed out, since

Chinese collective production units were created around small, preexisting natural units. The basic production and income-sharing unit consist[ed] not of specialized units spread over a wide area but of a production team of thirty or forty households in a single small village or neighborhood of some larger village. Peasants thus work[ed] and share[d] income with people who [were] their close neighbors and often their close kinsmen as well. . . . Besides incorporating old loyalties, these production units . . . generated new loyalties.[41]

Under Mao the state center's socialist goals theoretically favored promotion of larger and larger units of agricultural production and income sharing, to achieve both superior efficiency and fuller equity. But the center's pursuit of expanded or enlarged rural accounting units and income sharing arrangements that would not differentiate so sharply between families on the basis of the amount of labor they contributed met bitter peasant resistance in the late 1950s and again in the late 1960s and early 1970s. The smaller or lower forms of collectivization had coincided with and even reinforced peasant familist and localist cultural patterns. The very accomplishments of those little collective units seemed to make it more difficult for the center to impose "higher" or more "progressive" socialist goals on peasant communities. As Parish, whose research chronicled this process, concluded at the end of the decade of the 1970s, "The Chinese Communists have built a rural system that works fairly effectively, but one that constrains their ability to introduce further changes on all fronts at once."[42]

A similar example of the partial but interrupted integration of central and local values under Mao involves the selection and tenure of rural local leaders—production team and brigade cadres. One of the most important elements in the success of the party's early rural reform efforts was the deliberate policy of recruiting local leaders from within the villages to carry out the land reform and the establishment of collectives.[43] This technique, often contrasted with the Bolshevik Party's importation of urban outsiders to carry out similar tasks in the Soviet case, helped guarantee that, in China, the values and concerns of the original local community would be well reflected in the process of its reform and not stifled by the deluge of party rhetoric about the revolutionization of social relations. Locally recruited peasant village leaders did a great deal, then, to bridge the chasm of values between the party's simple rural class analysis and the local community's far more subtle, personalized criteria of honor, praise, and blame that, stretching back over many generations, yielded a local social stratification pattern embodying the community's most sacred values and judgments, and thus the context for meaningful self-definition in the future.

Team and brigade cadres continued to be recruited from within their villages all through the Mao era. They did not earn state salaries but were as dependent on the crop for their family income as were the other peasants they led. They were most unlikely to be promoted to jobs outside their locality, and so their standing in the community—local values and moral judgments—weighed as heavily on them as ever before. If the center then tried to impose policies in the villages that flew in the face of peasant norms and judgments, those local leaders were very frequently able to find both the courage and the means to resist. If pressed, they might even threaten to resign—a threat they were often only too pleased to carry out since the material and psychic rewards for the pains and privations of local leadership were dubious at best.[44] Thus, those village leaders may sometimes have acted as facilitators, but sometimes also as brakes on the further integration of central socialist and peasant localist norms and values.

If it wished, of course, the center was undeniably capable of training enormous pressures on peasant communities that deviated too far from the desired patriotic and socialist behavioral norms. The army, the police, and huge "work teams" swarming with radical party activists could, when necessary, be deployed to seize control of a village's affairs and to charge and bring punishment against offenders. Much more typically, however, most villages found themselves subjected only to periodic "clean-up" campaigns, rectification campaigns against "corrupt" local leaders, and a familiar barrage of propaganda/ education promoting revolutionary values and behavior. These campaigns were by no means without effect in the countryside. But if pressed too far they tended to alienate people and lead to mass resignations of valued local leaders. So, cadres and ordinary peasants generally deferred to the goals of the work teams and propaganda teams while they were actually in the villages. But once they left, it was recognized on both sides that targeted traditional attitudes and practices were almost certain gradually to reemerge.

By the late Mao era, then, there seems to be good reason to think that lines had already been drawn in the normative integration of revolutionary-socialist state center and peasant periphery. The state's own chosen rural administrative structures and routines, and the particular values and experiences characteristic of local cadres, appear to have contrived to set limits on the degree of effective normative integration attainable and sustainable in the villages. On this one of the three dimensions linking center and periphery, however, incomplete or interrupted integration was almost certainly not the result of conscious choice or preference on the part of central state leaders. On the contrary, there is every reason to think that the ultra-left leadership of the Cultural Revolution period genuinely sought (and somehow actually expected to attain) a true "unity of thought and will" that would encompass every Chinese citizen. But given other choices that had already been made concerning the institutions of governance and the economic organization of the peasant periphery, their ultimate deep frustration where normative integration was concerned may have been unavoidable. The cellular social structure and the segmentation of China's rural political economy confounded the would-be centralizers of thoughts and values, leaving the skeptical peasantry certainly to note, and perhaps to ponder, the many differences between people like themselves, who tried to avoid trouble and didn't pay much attention (*buguan*) to politics, and the sent-down youths and other urban-oriented outsiders who lived their dangerous lives in the searing light of Maoist political morality.

Conclusion

On all three of the integrative dimensions sketched here, we can see the imprint of the cellular structure of peasant social organization. On each dimension, the articulation of the center-periphery or state-society relationship under Mao reflected not only central goals, but also the organization and attitudes of salient groups at the periphery. Surveying these three dimensions suggests a complex, nonunitary pattern in the evolution of center-periphery (or state-society) relations.

In the sphere of *political/administrative integration* it appears that the center's seemingly deepest penetration of the periphery was in fact buffered through a criss-crossed network of horizontal and vertical offices that actually institutionalized, within the state structure itself, the segmentation of the rural periphery and the very tension between center and locality that continued to pervade Chinese society. In the sphere of *economic integration* it appears that the state center itself deliberately pursued policies strengthening the vertical segmentation of the periphery, finding in the ideal of self-reliant, comprehensive, but locally bounded economies a possible way out of some of its awesome economic development dilemmas. And in the sphere of *normative integration* it appears that peripheral units, having accommodated in part to central values, may yet have functioned effectively to deflect further normative penetration and to preserve a residual set of village values and ideals that coexisted alongside official formulations, setting limits to the process of their incorporation into mass society.

Residual peasant localism, and the related phenomenon of cadre departmentalism, may sometimes have been barriers and sometimes aids to central goals and actions. But peasant localism and rural cadre particularism appear always to have left their imprint on the evolving forms of social integration in Mao's China.

Thus in conclusion this preliminary discussion, which has employed a center-periphery approach, yields just two general hypotheses about the evolution of state-society relations under Chinese socialism. First, the vertical segmentation and localism of peasant society remained, even with the collectivization of agriculture, an important social-structural characteristic of the Chinese periphery, and a visible factor in all the major dimensions of social integration and of state-society relations. Second, the penetration of China's village periphery by its state socialist center was seldom, under Mao, unmediated and direct, and it may never have been as complete as the available models of the state socialist political phenomenon would lead us to expect.

If this, in turn, would seem to suggest a degree of local-level (and even village-level) autonomy in China, we must remember that it could only be a *relative* autonomy, liable to fluctuations, and encompassed within a larger reality of a party/state system which, in theory at least, admitted of few legitimate restraints on its power and authority at *any* level of administration. It is little surprise, perhaps, that such an ambitious state's reach frequently exceeded its actual grasp on local affairs. These general hypotheses are therefore intended not merely to draw attention to the existence of a certain relative autonomy within the system, but to point the way toward an analysis of its origins, forms, and patterns in the evolving postrevolutionary polity. And they point toward the resilient social structures and social ideals of China's vast peasantry, as those structures and ideals interacted with the party/state's own socialist aspirations and policies, as a promising starting point for such an analysis.

These are broad hypotheses, resting here only on sketches of the arguments that would confirm them. If they prove valuable in future research it will be, in my view, because of the widespread influence up to now of the counterfactual belief that state socialist systems would arise in mostly industrialized and urbanized environments. This is a belief that ironically has been shared by many European and Third World socialist theorists, on the one hand, who have seemed never able to rid themselves of futuristic visions of abundance and attendant social order; and by anti-communists on the other hand, who see totalitarian penetration and control as the hidden agenda of all socialist experiments. No doubt, in a largely urban-industrial environment, with sophisticated rapid mass communications, extensive unified markets, and rationalized bureaucratic organizations, the theoretical potential for tight social integration is indeed great. And so it has generally been on drawing boards already strewn with sketches of such a tightly integrated industrial social formation that both totalitarian theorists and socialist planners have penciled in their respective myths about socialist transformation. China, however, was and still is a mostly agrarian, largely peasant society, not an industrial or urban one. The depth of the agrarian periphery and of primordial peasant localism remained too palpable under Mao to be wished away. Chinese socialist state builders of the Mao era seem to have looked instead for ways "to domesticate" localist loyalties, to incorporate them into state socialist structures, and turn them, where possible, into a positive force for socialist development.[45] The form and intensity of village-state relations, as well as the continually evolving pattern of national social integration under Mao, were profoundly affected by this acknowledgement of China's agrarian social basis.

Three

The Reach of
the State

*A Comparative-Historical
Approach to the "Modernization"
of Local Government in China*

In modern times bureaucratization and social leveling within political, and particularly within state organizations in connection with the destruction of feudal and local privileges have very frequently benefited the interests of capitalism. Often bureaucratization has been carried out in direct alliance with capitalist interests, for example, the great historical alliance of the power of the absolute prince with capitalist interests. In general, a legal leveling and destruction of firmly established local structures ruled by notables has usually made for a wider range of capitalist activity. Yet one may expect as an effect of bureaucratization, a policy that meets the petty bourgeois interest in a secured traditional "subsistence," or even a state socialist policy that strangles opportunities for private profit. This has occurred in several cases of historical and far-reaching importance, specifically during antiquity; it is undoubtedly to be expected as a future development. MAX WEBER

Contemporary commentary and analysis, emanating from both China and the West, often suggests or assumes that the reforms of the post-Mao period represent, in essence, a healthy retreat by the overweening socialist state apparatus from its prior posture of excessive intrusion into social life. Today's reformers, we are given to understand, have learned from their own bitter experience how cruel and counterproductive it can be for socialists to try to control too much with the stunning hammerblows of bureaucracy and the stinging cattle-prods of ideology corroded by cult of personality. We may be reassured, then, that in the contemporary Chinese state-society relationship, the state is at long last backing down.

Perhaps. And yet, one of the leading governmental reform slogans in Beijing all along has been the one that advises, "Control less, in order to control it better." Simple prudence, therefore, cautions skepticism regarding any "destatization" hypothesis. Obviously, whether we believe we are now catching the state in the act of retreat or in the act of reorganization and reconsolidation will depend largely on how we have conceived the nature and dimensions of the actual Chinese state-society relationship in the recent past.

In the first two decades after the revolution, Western observers tended to be struck by the evident increase in state power in China under the People's Republic. The elaboration of a party/state cadre network that reached into the remotest rural hamlets, the spectacle of swift collectivization, the Great Leap Forward, and other mass mobilization efforts all created the impression abroad that there was practically nothing the Chinese state could not do. As one colleague recently expressed this view, it seemed possible "to pick up the phone in Beijing and make any decision stick down in the village." More recently, however, analysts of Chinese politics have tended to dwell on what the contemporary state was (and is) *unable* to do, and why. No longer do we see the bureaucracy and the cadre network as mechanical transmission belts, ready and willing to convey central decisions to the periphery without deviation. Vested interests, political opinion groups, and personal networks intertwine to make the structure of the Chinese state highly complex and certainly not univocal. Researchers now routinely stress that when, in the course of policy implementation, this byzantine structure confronts villagers and village cadres, who have agendas of their own, the political outcome is usually not the instant compliance that so often appears on the polished surface of the polity.

"Totalitarian" assumptions about the omniscient and omnipotent state have yielded to messier descriptions of intrabureaucratic politics and inconclusive state-society interactions. We can now discern a variety of institutionally and geographically demarcated zones of politics in which wily lower-level politicians pursue evasive, defensive, and sometimes aggressive strategies that frequently confound central intentions. Few would dispute the center's ability to mobilize the crushing coercive power of the state against those who would disobey. Yet everyday Chinese politics in recent decades is now understood to have been as often marked by negotiation and bargaining as by the threat or use of coercion, still less by mechanical obedience.

If the state-society relationship in China has not been so absolutely state-dominated as earlier supposed, then careful distinctions must be made in analyzing the alleged "retreat" of the state under Deng's reforms. Specifically, do the reforms and restructurings remove only the intrusive mechanisms of socialist politics and state power? Or do they also weaken certain protective and defensive mechanisms, bargains, patterns, and routines that enabled local communities and other social units sometimes to thwart central control? Most observers would agree that the stridently "politicized state" of the Cultural Revolution era has mercifully adopted a lower profile under Deng. But whether the reforms will ultimately shorten the effective reach of China's busy "administrative state" remains uncertain at best. To highlight the uncertainties, this essay explores some of the real (but often hidden) limitations on the reach of the state that prevailed in rural China in the recent past. For additional insight, analogies and comparisons are drawn with selected aspects of China's long history of bureaucratic administration. Only at the end do we return to speculation about the effects of the present effort to modernize and reform China's system of local government. The thrust of the argument is to show that in some respects, the sociopolitical changes accompanying the "liberal market" reforms of the 1980s may impair the ability of peasant communities to oppose inimical state actions and policies. Ironically perhaps, the "reform" order may render some rural villagers more rather than less vulnerable to the designs of outside powerholders. Risk is the certain companion of uncertain freedom.

Preview of the Argument

The Deng Xiaoping coalition of the 1980s wants to "modernize" China's rural local government and administrative apparatus. The first wave of agricultural reforms after the Third Plenum involved commodity prices, household contracts, rural free markets, and other important modifications of economic policy and line. The second wave of reforms, however, has targeted the very structure, staffing, and operating ethos of local government.[1] Today's leaders want to break up the previous "fused" form of commune administration, for example. They seek to separate local economic decisionmaking authority from village civil government functions, and reorganize rural economic activity into new companies, combines, and corporations.[2] They intend to break down many old rural administrative units, merging them into new economic zones, under the authority of nearby towns or cities. They aim for a big turnover in the rural cadre force, easing out old line party regulars and bringing in younger specialists whose "problem orientation" will be more technical, less personal, and less political. They are designing new salary and bonus systems to induce rural cadres to behave more like company employees and corporate executives than like guardians of the revolutionary mass line.

All these reforms, taken in the name of modernizing China's state and economy, are buttressed and justified by a wholesale and penetrating critique of the Maoist past. This contemporary indictment of the rural political economic system, at least since the Great Leap Forward, claims that China's peasants had been laboring under a tyranny at once hypercentralized, brutally inflexible, arbitrary, *and also* fragmented, irrationally personalistic, and corrupt. Students of recent Chinese history immediately recognize some truth on both sides of this seeming antinomy. Yet, could China under Mao and the Communist Party have been both too centralized and too decentralized? Hyperstatized and yet politically parcelized?[3]

The central thesis of this essay is that in the early traditional Chinese polity, the competition between the ambitions of imperial statebuilders and the prerogatives of the landed elite was not resolved in the same manner as in Western Europe; nor for that matter did the ancient Chinese empire follow the Russian and East European "late bloomers'" path to modern statehood. China had never experienced the profound political fragmentation of European feudalism; had never succumbed completely to centrifugal forces of the kind that so elaborately parcelized political authority during the West's long Middle Ages. Therefore, paradoxically perhaps, the practitioners of Confucian statecraft were never to subdue and transcend the remaining (and resilient) centrifugal, parcelizing tendencies within their own polity as decisively as did the builders of the Western absolutist states. China's early military conquerors and emperors had reached a different *modus vivendi* with their locally dominant landowners that eventually produced a historically discrete class—the Chinese gentry. For most of its long history, the "gentry" kept one foot in the state bureaucracy and the other firmly on the land. It held up the empire, but also kept alive the unending struggle between central authority and local control that remained the dominant *problematic* of governance in China from Qin times through the 1911 revolution, and beyond.

Many givens of Chinese politics were decisively overturned when the Communist Party came to power, but the abiding tension between state center and locality was not one of these. Central-local struggle was, in fact, reinstitutionalized in the interlocking vertical (*tiao tiao*) and horizontal (*kuai kuai*) gridwork of the postrevolutionary party/state apparatus. And as for the party's network of rural cadres, though in many important respects they differed vastly from the old local gentry, pressed as they became by the structure and the expectations of the new administrative system to act at once as agents of the state and defenders of their regions, they frequently adopted a dual role not unlike that of certain segments of the old regime elites. As with the gentry, local party cadres have endured now blame by the center, now hostility from the people, for their perceived lapses of loyalty to one side or the other. Thus, the lofty contemporary edifice of state socialism in China rests on imperial pilings of great antiquity. And like bats chattering high up in the belfries of this structure, today's political struggles and bargains bear a haunting resemblance to ghostly ancestors long buried below.

But there is more to this essay's purpose than simply to note once again that the legacies of China's long history can be detected in the workings of her contemporary polity. For that ingenious deadlock between central and local power which manifested itself in the astounding longevity of the Chinese gentry has also been associated with what many historians have regarded as China's greatest historical dilemma. The traditional Chinese scholar-gentry, aside from its reputation for fine calligraphy, blatant corruption, and melancholy drunkenness and poeticism by moonlight, has primarily been noted, by Chinese and Western interpreters alike, for its historical inability to move the Chinese economy beyond mercantilism to capitalism. Members of China's landed and lettered gentry may cheerfully have entered commerce and business entrepreneurship and may well have prospered under the tendency toward state mercantilism during the late empire, but unlike landed elites in the West, they did not transform themselves into a freestanding bourgeoisie. Instead, even late into the last dynasty, this class worked most skillfully to maintain its own firm and deliberate occupation of the crucial nexus between agricultural production and state surplus extraction. Here is the source of its special reputation for profound social and economic conservatism. Social theorists, noting the gentry's capacity for vigorous class self-perpetuation and self-renewal in the roles of rural local governance and control, have charged it with actually having stood in the way of an economic developmental breakthrough to capitalism and urban industrialism.[4]

China's latter-day local elites, her village cadres, are now implicitly accused by the Deng Xiaoping forces of playing the same kind of obstructionist role under socialism. Cadre "localism," the argument goes, contrived with certain elements of ultra-left Maoist thought to produce primitivist limitations on commodity specialization, commercial exchange, and the growth of market towns, thus deepening rural stagnation rather than spurring investment for a developmental take-off into industrialism. The goal of the Deng Xiaoping coalition is to transcend the ancient central-local *problematic* of governance. They want to eliminate the networks of conservative localist protectionism that, in the Marxist vocabulary, are associated with China's precapitalist or "feudal" past. They want to replace the privileged but parochial old comrades' elite of the countryside with a corps of apolitical technocrats. And they say they want to loosen statist controls over economic life by expanding the role of the market. Meanwhile they propose to transcend the cellularity of village and local marketing communities through crop specialization, agricultural commodification, and the development of rural-urban integrated commercial networks on a scale China has not previously experienced.

In this light, the contemporary reformers no doubt see themselves as simultaneously attacking the hypertrophy of the "modern" state under twentieth-century socialism *and* the intransigent personalism and fragmentation of a "premodern" political system that had persisted even under Mao. In this light also it becomes clear why both the structure and the ethos of China's rural local government must now be a focus of vigorous reform and "modernization." As argued below, however, while the Deng coalition's critique of the Maoist past contains many telling points, its commercializing design for the future seems bound to betray its anti-statist promise.

Statemaking

Three aspects of imperial China's prodigious statemaking effort merit special attention here: its historical precociousness and institutional continuity; its "conquer, civilize, and control" mentality; and its deep dependence on the gentry symbiosis of landed interests and officialdom. These three aspects will allow some interesting contrasts with European statemaking patterns.

As a practical matter, we date Chinese imperial history from 221 B.C., the founding of the Qin empire, even if certain important institutions of state had their origins much earlier, at the ascendancy of the Western Zhou (1122 to 771 B.C.).[5]

Between 500 and 211 B.C., with its capital at Xianyang, the Qin state rulers expanded their territory through systematic conquest of neighboring states and non-Han tribes. First they subdued the state of Shu in the Chinese interior. By 250 B.C. they had captured Wei and Han to the east. And in the next thirty years they swept over the states of Zhao, Yan, Song, Qi, and Chu to take complete command of the eastern and northern coastal regions of the Chinese mainland. Finally, by 211 B.C., Qin's mounted archers patrolled a large area in the south as well, driving through to the coast near present-day Guangzhou. And like statemakers in other parts of the world, for whom warfare is, as Machiavelli wrote, "the only art expected of a ruler," they continued fighting—the Xiongnu in the north, the Yue in the south.

The unitary Qin state conscripted peasants for military service and built the first major irrigation and transport canals. The Qin emperor also inaugurated another important statemaking tradition in China—the dogged effort to neutralize locally based challenges to central authority. In 213 B.C. he ordered the destruction of local records, "a deliberate act of policy aimed at extinguishing local loyalties."[6]

The Qin state was quickly succeeded by the Han, which built more dikes and transport canals to carry grain taxes to the capital. Han emperors levied heavier taxes on merchants and established state monopolies in iron, salt, and wine, thereby making the Chinese state both more imposing and more of an imposition on its people. The alert Emperor Wu (140–87 B.C.) paid special attention to rebellious rumblings from the regional aristocracy, rumblings he could not but interpret as threatening to central dynastic control. On apparently trumped-up charges, he confiscated the lands of 127 Han princes, turning the state itself into China's largest landowner by the end of the second century B.C. Under the Han dynasty the state regularly distributed public land to poor people "to counterbalance the growth of great estates"[7] and to establish a stable yeoman peasantry, grateful to the central government, on the land. Finally, the celebrated "well-field system" promoted by Wang Mang, who usurped the Han throne in A.D. 9, along with his other (ultimately unsuccessful) attempts to abolish the market in land and slaves, marked the most supremely ambitious effort of China's early statemakers to limit the power and scope of landed interests.

Thus, the political leitmotif of central-local struggle was sounded early in Chinese history. But Wang Mang's reign was short, and the later Han emperors owed the restoration of their dynasty to a coalition of magnates. Under pressure of fighting "barbarian" tribes, quelling now more frequent peasant uprisings and putting down the Yellow Turban rebels, these magnates gathered economic strength and retainers and turned themselves gradually into local militarists. The central state's system of conscription collapsed, and the once glorious Han had to rely more and more on warlord armies, "amnestied convicts, and above all on barbarian auxiliaries" to defend itself.[8] With the breakdown of the Han, China entered three hundred years of intermittent war and "barbarian" absorption, during which the landed aristocratic families enjoyed a resurgence. Yet this resurgence fell short of genuinely feudal entrenchment. As Patricia Ebrey has concluded in her interesting study of aristocracy during the unsettled period after the fall of the Han,

> both complaints of the power of the aristocratic families and boasts of their own eminence must be interpreted in a specifically Chinese context. . . . [A]ristocratic families had exceptionally secure prestige and power in comparison to elite groups in other periods of Chinese history, yet they never gained a cultural, political, or economic base as sound as the most aristocratic groups in European or Japanese history. . . . [D]espite the extensive damage inflicted on the social and political order, Han values, ideals, and institutions were never totally discredited. Thus, families . . . who were at the top of provincial society aspired toward association with the court.[9]

This "eagerness to be associated with the imperial court" was already part of the tradition of the Chinese aristocracy:

Although they had adequate private resources to hold themselves aloof from antagonistic rulers, the long-established ideal of the gentleman-official retained its strength; whenever practicable aristocrats sought prestigious court positions. This attitude seems to have effectively countered any tendencies for the aristocratic families to become feudal lords with proprietary control over sections of the country.[10]

The diffusion of power was severe when the Han dynasty collapsed, and at other periods of Chinese history yet to come. But the ideals of gentlemanly service to the ruler and of the glory of the unified empire were not lost.[11] The Chinese heartland would indeed have to be conquered and unified all over again. But with the eventual rise of the Tang state in 618, even more effective means for managing central-local tensions were to be put in place.

By the mid-seventh century, Tang emperors were selecting some of their high state officials through public examination. The examination system acquired such prestige that even the sons of magnates put themselves forward as candidates. The military segment of the state's apparatus simultaneously lost much of its governing role and social status, and the signal creation of Chinese imperial civilization, the scholarly civilian bureaucracy, was born. There would be many more military usurpers and conquering nomadic armies, of course, but China's lettered civilian bureaucratic tradition was to endure. Throughout the Tang and Song epochs the state bureaucracy grew and became increasingly differentiated. Study for the examinations became far more rigorous and the average age of successful candidates rose into the mid-thirties. More and more central state and provincial offices were occupied by degree-holders. And the censorate was erected to serve as watchdog over the whole.

Interestingly, the florescence of the civil bureaucracy in Tang and Song times was matched by an actual decline in the state's direct control over land. The early Tang state claimed for itself final authority over the disposition of all land, and it administered an "equal field" system of lifetime (but mostly nonheritable) grants of land to farm families.[12] At least in the non-rice-growing north, this system seems to have been remarkably well enforced. But after the protracted effort to put down the An Lushan rebellion, larger private estates did in fact emerge once again, often owned by civil officials and bureaucrats. By Song times, the state in theory was still sole proprietor of all land, but private ownership of agricultural tracts, from tiny farms to extensive estates, had become the norm in the Chinese social order.[13]

The connection seems clear. The Tang empire employed the examination system and the expansion of the civil bureaucracy to neutralize and co-opt the military aristocracy and to incorporate those potentially dangerous families into the central state establishment. The threat that private estate-holding would lead to entrenched parcelization of power was perceived to fade when the noble warrior ethic was overwhelmed by the learned ideal of the Confucian statesman. The imperial Chinese state could afford not to have direct control of land if it could control its major landowners by other means. With the Song, therefore, the complex social formation known as the Chinese "gentry" had come into its own.[14]

The precise social reference of the term "gentry" (*shen-shih*) has been a matter of much puzzlement and dispute among historians of China. Ho Ping-ti, for example, confines the meaning of "gentry" to "the class of officials and potential officials" who, "during a greater part of the Ming-Ch'ing period, owed their status only partly to wealth but mostly to an academic degree." This is a bureaucratically rooted and rather strict definition, especially since Ho specifically excludes the *sheng-yuan*, the numerous holders of the first or lowest scholarly degree.[15] Chang Chung-li, on the other hand, divides the "gentry" into an upper and a lower stratum, assigning all types of *sheng-yuan* and all holders of purchased degrees to the lower stratum and including in the upper stratum only holders of official rank (whether purchased or appointed) and those scholars who had earned higher degrees.[16] Thus, for Chang, possessing official rank and earning a degree through examination were the two criteria of gentry status, and under most conditions either one by itself was sufficient.

In his treatment of the *shen-shih* concept, Frederic Wakeman accepts the distinction between upper and lower degree-holders, between the "official gentry" and the "scholar gentry," but argues for still another source of gentry status, pointing to "certain other kinds of local notables whose families were regarded as . . . eminent lineages of a high social pedigree":

> Indeed those households, even if devoid of degree-holders, apparently also belonged to what would be regarded by contemporaries as the local gentry of a county. Consequently, one sees only half the picture when . . . defining gentry membership solely in terms of degrees conferred by the imperial government. . . . By the Ch'ing period, *shih* was loosely used to describe leading members of the local elite who were not necessarily *shen* (degree-holders). Magistrates' handbooks defined them as "heads of the masses," and singled them out as being "exactly the ones to rely upon in persuading the people to follow the instructions of the officials." As *shih*, the gentry was not just the ascribed creation of the state; it held an independent status of its own because of local prestige which was based upon wealth, education, power, and influence.[17]

Thus, looked at somewhat more broadly, the dominant class of traditional China might best be regarded as consisting of the *official-gentry*, the *scholar-gentry*, and the *local notable (or lower) gentry*. Obviously, in normal times there was considerable overlap, and both upward and downward mobility, among these subgroups.[18] Wakeman's less exclusive definition highlights this very eclectic and fluid reality of gentry rule, especially in the sphere of local governance, and so it is adopted here. Indeed, an important part of the analysis to come depends on being able to distinguish between those members of the gentry holding office in, and those gentry families simply resident in, a given locality. As an internally stratified, not always cohesive, yet highly self-conscious social class, the gentry embodied the mutual interests and interdependence of the imperial state and the agrarian elite.

This local notable-scholar-official synthesis by no means eliminated the struggle between state center and locality. Rather, it concentrated the tension within itself and contained the struggle in an overarching framework of alliance: an alliance to preserve both the state's ability to extract some surplus from the land and the landed elite's interest in domestic peace and the social status quo. From Tang and Song times, throughout China's long imperial history, this compound gentry would be more or less constantly embroiled in central-local political maneuvering, sometimes shoring up the central state and sometimes pulling away from it. But with its ever-dual loyalty to its home base and the metropolitan bureaucratic culture, the gentry continued to serve as the glue that held together and repeatedly repaired the broken pieces of China's prodigious polity.

This analysis of the Chinese gentry's ambiguous identity and dual loyalty differs from the picture that has been drawn by some of our most learned historians. Etienne Balazs, for example, likened "the imperial Chinese regime" to Western absolutism, and even to totalitarianism, and depicted the scholar-bureaucrats as willing tools of the emperor and unrelenting enemies of local particularist tendencies and other challenges to the throne:

There can surely be no other ruling class to compare with the mandarinate for capacity to survive, wealth of experience, and success in the art of governing. It is true that as rulers they cost the Chinese people dear. The strait jacket into which the scholar officials forced the amorphous body of China was agonizingly uncomfortable, and inflicted innumerable frustrations and sufferings. Yet this costly contraption served a necessary purpose. It was the price paid for the homogeneity, long duration, and vitality of Chinese civilization. As many an episode in Chinese history has shown, if it had not been for the scholar officials, acting as benign shepherds and keeping the feudalists in order . . . while maintaining an iron control on the unity of the empire, particularism would have won the day, and, with the breakup of sovereignty, Chinese civilization would have collapsed altogether. The fact that the mandarins' motives were not disinterested made no difference to the final outcome.[19]

Against this, we have Albert Feuerwerker's depiction in his excellent monograph on the Qing polity:

> the complex of political institutions centering on the emperor and his bureaucracy represented only one-half of the Chinese political synthesis. The long-lived and much remarked political stability should be seen as the product of a continuing equilibrium between institutions that can be described as tending in the direction of universalism and specificity and emanating from the political center, and a competing or overlapping set emanating from the local governmental and kinship level that tended in the direction of particularism and diffuseness.

And further on:

> The long life of China's traditional political institutions may be seen, in part, as the product of an equilibrium in tension between these two levels of the polity. Whatever the claims of Peking, government of a country of China's size and population from a single center and by means of detailed prescriptive regulations—what one today would call a centralized authoritarian state—was an impossibility before the twentieth century, if for no other reason than because premodern technology, especially in the means of communication, ruled it out of the question. Conversely, a political system founded entirely on the above-mentioned local complex of institutions would simply not provide an adequate basis for subcontinent wide political integration. *Both hemispheres were needed: the problem was to see that they fitted properly, a problem that runs through the whole of China's imperial history.*[20]

Here Feuerwerker, if only obliquely, addresses the essential ambivalence of the gentry's position in the polity.[21] Balazs speaks of imperial bureaucrats as if they approached Weberian rationality, and therefore he dismisses their individual and group interests as of no account in the pattern of historical development. But Feuerwerker takes special note of the locality-based interests and values that were continually impinging on the centrally organized governing apparatus. He conceives of these as the lower "hemisphere" of the Chinese political order, and with this metaphor he is able to suggest both the essential complementarity and the inescapable tension between the two halves of the imperial Chinese polity. He comes much closer to capturing what we might well regard as the distinctive element in the Chinese approach to governance: a synthesis that effectively *forestalled the necessity* of a decisive transition from the honeycomb polity of premodern particularism to the centrally coordinated and penetrating networks of modern statism. Adapting the terminology historians apply to the Western world, then, we might say that in late imperial China a *no longer feudal* base was linked to a *not fully elaborated* centralized bureaucracy. China's Janus-faced gentry inhabited the middle ground, reading the signals from both cultural complexes.

Before going on to look more closely at exactly how the gentry mediated between center and locality, we can summarize what has been said so far about China's statemaking experience with the help of some comparisons to the West. This seems worth attempting, even when mindful of the difficulties and dangers such comparison entails.[22]

China never experienced Western Europe's ornate chains of rear vassalage and subinfeudation, manorialism, parcelized sovereignties and scalar properties, all legitimized, indeed sanctified, by holy ritual and other churchly intercessions. For a thousand years, from the fall of the West Roman Empire to the end of the fifteenth century, despite the wars of Charlemagne and other would-be emperors, Europe remained profoundly fragmented. Time, distance, and the limits of available technology permitted the deep entrenchment of local jurisdictions and traditional sovereignties. When the builders of Tang sought to reestablish central state authority they could still see their task, as had their Qin (and Roman) precursors, primarily as one of subduing rebellious lords and pacifying non-Han peoples on the edges of civilization. Europe's modern statebuilders, by contrast, looked out over no such seemingly wild and empty periphery. Elaborated over centuries, genuine feudalism opposed them with highly intricate and morally recognized patterns of rights, loyalties, and preferments.[23] Charles Tilly makes the contrast:

> Unlike the Chinese and Roman state-builders of earlier times, the Europeans of 1500 and later did not ordinarily expand from a highly organized center into a weakly organized periphery. . . . Indeed, building substantial states in much of Europe meant absorbing numerous political units which already exercised significant claims to sovereignty—free cities, principalities, bishoprics, and a variety of other entities. The European state-makers engaged in the work of combining, consolidating, neutralizing, manipulating a tough, complicated, and well-set web of political relations. They sought to fashion something larger and stronger than had existed before. In order to accomplish that, they had to tear or dissolve large parts of the web, and to face furious resistance as they did so.[24]

Tilly's reference to free cities raises another important contrast between the patterns of European feudalism and the Chinese case. There was room in the Western feudal matrix for the development of relatively autonomous cities, of identifiably urban interests and urban classes.[25] As Perry Anderson has argued, free towns and a mercantile bourgeoisie were natural accompaniments to Western feudalism's demesne farming and patchwork sovereignty:

> The mediaeval town had been able to develop because the hierarchical dispersal of sovereignties in the feudal mode of production for the first time freed urban economies from direct domination by a rural ruling class. The towns in this sense were never exogenous to feudalism in the West . . . in fact, the very condition of their existence was the unique "de-totalization" of sovereignty within the politico-economic order of feudalism.[26]

Anderson, of course, is concerned to revise the general view of Marx and Engels that the Western absolutist states were the creations of the rising class, the bourgeoisie. Quite the contrary, he says: "Absolutism was essentially . . . *a redeployed and recharged apparatus of feudal domination* . . .

in other words, the Absolutist State was never an arbiter between the aristocracy and the bourgeoisie, still less an instrument of the nascent bourgeoisie against the aristocracy: it was the new political carapace of a threatened nobility."[27] The merchants of early modern Europe would surely have preferred laissez-faire to the state mercantile philosophy of a Bodin or Colbert. The rising state did not always serve the "rising class" very well. Nevertheless, the very existence of the mediaeval towns and the rapid growth of the bourgeoisie did affect the developing forms of Western absolutism. According to Anderson, a provident "field of compatibility" emerged between the interests of the monarchy and those of mercantile and manufacturing capital. "Economic centralization, protectionism and overseas expansion aggrandized the . . . State while they profited the early bourgeoisie. They increased the taxable revenues of the one by providing business opportunities for the other."[28] This cooperation gave the bourgeoisie a certain voice within the state and prevented the landed nobility from consolidating its preferred "regressive solution" in the protracted class struggle taking place on the land.[29]

Practically none of this resonates with the Chinese experience, however. The early modern state of Tang arose without benefit of the full fragmentation of genuine feudalism, and thus without benefit of free cities of the sort that flourished at the interstices of the Western feudal network. Historians of China do not usually speak of large commercial centers much before the end of Tang and early Song, and then, like Jacques Gernet, they quickly come to focus on the state's trade monopolies. Gernet cites the late Tang agricultural, commercial, and urban expansion, attributing it to progress in wet-rice cultivation, the development of trade routes linking the lower Yangzi and Sichuan with the north, and to the development of new commercial techniques like the negotiable certificate of deposit, which was later to give birth to the banknote. But he concludes with this observation: "In this context, the establishment of state monopolies favored the rise of a new class of great merchants, who were, however, unable to escape from the guardianship of those with political power."[30]

Or, in the stronger language of Etienne Balazs:

> I must insist, as Max Weber did . . . , on the negative factors accounting for the arrested development of towns and of an urban class in the East and particularly in China. These are, in the first place, the absence of charters, of legalized status, of a system of jurisprudence, and, above all, of a code of civil law. Next, there was the lack of civil liberty, of secure privileges, and of autonomy in the administration of towns, so that the towns—unlike those of the West—did not become a magnet for the countryside. The town was therefore unable to fill the role of social catalyst. Unlike our towns, it could not become the center of attraction because its life remained dominated, as indeed the entire social organism was dominated, by the omnipresent and omnipotent state—that is, the uncontested, absolute, and despotic power of a class of scholar-officials who could not tolerate any form of private enterprise, or who seized any private undertaking that had by chance succeeded in flourishing, in order to stifle it.[31]

Again Balazs goes too far in speaking of the state's "uncontested omnipotence"; but was he also incorrect in dwelling on the retardant role played by China's special forms of mutual cooptation between the nonofficial gentry and the state bureaucracy?

Newer waves of Japanese and Western research have indeed been chipping away at the rather undifferentiated depiction of the place of China's cities and of her urban commercial elites in the processes of historical change, typified here by the writings of Balazs. In William Rowe's notable study of nineteenth century Hankou, the several points at issue in the interpretive debate about Chinese cities have been addressed most forcefully. Hankou was, by Rowe's own admission, not a typical Chinese entrepôt but a "vanguard locality."[32] Yet he uses the Hankou case to argue quite compellingly that by the end of the late Qing, the widening scope of guild action and authority had yielded an important degree of urban autonomy in at least some Chinese cities, even without the peculiarly Western device of the municipal charter:

The state's monopoly of ideological orthodoxy (by consensus of the elite), combined with an extremely low level of effective governmental penetration of the society, meant that for substantive urban autonomy to be achieved it was unnecessary, indeed undesirable, to provoke legalistic confrontations—by demanding municipal charters, for example. Rather, in the interstices of the imperial system there was ample leeway for local self-reliance, urban as well as rural.

In nineteenth-century Hankow, it seems, there was an unusually wide gap between de jure and de facto systems of political authority. Thus a substantial degree of de facto autonomy had emerged, with real power balanced between officials and the leaders of local society; over the century the balance shifted very much toward the latter.[33]

Even through the eyes of revisionist historians like Rowe, then, as Qing authority and bureaucratic capacity dramatically decayed at the close of the nineteenth century and an authentic urban consciousness and autonomy were on the rise, the "state's monopoly on ideological orthodoxy" upheld "by consensus of the elite" still remained in place, the keystone of the enduring polity. An independent and coherent "bourgeois" social philosophy did not emerge, it appears, even in vanguard Hankou.[34] The absence of a specifically bourgeois social value system, a bourgeois political ideology and agenda, appears to have kept even the rapidly rising urban commercialism of the late Qing within the familiar bounds of state mercantile, not capitalist, activity.[35]

In the absence of a specifically bourgeois social philosophy and political agenda, the municipal consciousness and autonomy scholars are now documenting still remain comfortably comprehensible within the ancient *problematic* of central-local power competition and—to use Rowe's word—balance. The new scholarship clearly shows a previously unappreciated complexity of social stratification (internal to the "gentry") and a previously unappreciated intensity of social differentiation emerging around urban commercial enterprise in the last decades of the imperial period; but it has not yet shown for China the kind of "class politics" that would truly have heralded an economic and sociopolitical breakthrough to the complex we call capitalist modernism.[36]

To return to our summary comparison, then, the centralized Chinese state took shape *very early*, not by making combinations of already acknowledged customary jurisdictions but by territorial conquest using towns as waystations and radiating beacons of its civilizing authority. Chinese statemakers made their major class alliance with the landed warrior nobility, and successfully coopted that group through the civil service examination system. Members of the gentry functioned simultaneously as public revenue collectors, private and family entrepreneurs, and patrons on the land. In this way the gentry's special synthesis of local village notables, city-based commercial elites, scholars and office-holding bureaucrats formed a dominant class that bridged rural *and* urban China. This amorphous group absorbed within itself virtually all the potential conflicts between urban proto-capitalists, landed elites, and the state. It accomplished this feat of harmonization by (a) maintaining its own control in the lower hemisphere of governance, i.e., mediating between the state and the landed classes in the act of agricultural surplus extraction; and (b) pursuing sometimes extraordinarily ambitious *mercantile* ventures for private and state enrichment, but *stopping short of a transition to manufacturing capitalism*, averting the rise of a powerful, free-standing, urban bourgeoisie.[37]

The territory of late imperial China was by no means an uninterrupted rural expanse of herders and cultivators. Small towns and great cities flourished, offering new avenues for investment, new arenas for the exercise of power, and new social units with which to link one's own identity. Successful and powerful gentry families naturally gravitated to urban centers, often leaving their farmlands in the hands of managers, and over the generations adopting a more metropolitan point of view.[38] Nevertheless, even the most powerful and financially diversified gentry families tended to retain their roots in the land of a specific locality. And in localities without such exalted native families, effective management of local affairs tended to remain in the hands of native *lower* gentry figures. In this manner, localism and territoriality remained keys to Chinese politics, even into modern times. And when the last dynasty was to fall it was, not surprisingly, at the hands of provincial separatists and territorial militarists, whose brief and inglorious adventures were succeeded by the even greater fragmentation of the warlord era. When the glue finally came unstuck, the fault lines that yawned open still ran mostly along local or territorial, not socioeconomic, boundaries. The imperial gentry-official synthesis left China in 1911 with a long history of "localist" politics and with what Maurice Meisner has provocatively called a "weak" class structure.[39]

Rural Gentry and Local Governance

Here I will attempt to narrow our frame of vision and, leaving aside consideration of the *upper* gentry's official, commercial, and other occupations, turn instead to a more sustained assessment of the *lower* gentry's style and workaday roles in the task of rural local governance. The following summary by Fei Xiaotong is a good place to begin:

I hope to have made certain points clear. . . . (1) In the traditional Chinese power structure there were two different layers: on the top, the central government; at the bottom, the local governing unit whose leaders were the gentry class. (2) There was a *de facto* limit to the authority of the central government. Local affairs, managed in the community by the gentry, were hardly interfered with by the central authorities. (3) Legally there was only one track—from the top down—along which passed imperial orders. But in actual practice, by the use of intermediaries such as the government servants . . . , unreasonable orders might be turned back. This influence from the bottom up is not usually recognized in discussions of the formal governmental institutions of China, but it was effective nevertheless.[40]

According to Fei, the combination of the informal power of the lower (or "local notable") gentry families and the formal power of those "official gentry" posted to serve in a given locality often contrived to create a zone of local politics not penetrated by central government power. This, the lower hemisphere of the polity, not only set limits on what the center could successfully demand, it also sometimes influenced higher-level decisionmaking. How, exactly, did the "official gentry/local notable gentry" synthesis work to this end of restraining central control?

For analytical purposes, a modest typology of *the local governing roles and behaviors* of the lower gentry can be employed to distinguish between (a) roles that primarily served the interests of the state, (b) roles that primarily served the interests of the lower gentry families themselves, and (c) roles that primarily served the interests of their rural community. In actuality these roles were usually intimately intertwined, and the effort to separate them here should only serve to highlight the more fundamental reality: *China's traditional rural order rested on a conscious fusion of economy, society, and polity, on the basis of locality and by means of interlocked networks of formal and informal ties.*

(a) *Roles primarily serving the state.* Local notable or lower gentry families were most conspicuously involved in assisting the state in the work of surplus extraction from their locality, i.e., in tax collection and the organization of corvée labor services. They also played the role of the "eyes and ears" of the county magistrate, providing information about neighbors, other residents, and suspicious persons passing through. In this way, and by their efforts to raise and maintain a local militia, they assisted the state in its policing functions and in the maintenance of social order.[41] Notable local families and poor but honorable local scholars also served the state as public examples and guardians of Confucianism, the official state philosophy. By living their public lives approximately in accord with the ritual demanded by Confucian learning, by engaging

Confucian scholar tutors for their sons, and by delivering an occasional *xiangyue* lecture for the edification of the assembled masses, they affirmed the moral order on which the state rested its claim to legitimacy.[42]

However, in their support of the state in these three areas of surplus extraction, maintenance of social order, and celebration of the official moral code, the lower gentry often were able also both to enrich themselves *and* to defend the community against certain state demands. The state bureaucracy had little if any means by which to supervise or sanction members of local gentry families in their performance of these essential services. For all its grandeur, China's imperial bureaucracy did not directly penetrate into the rural local community. Mandarin officials, always non-natives, were posted only as far down as the county seat.[43] They surveyed the *terra incognita* that was theirs to administer (where often they could not even understand the local dialect), and they necessarily leaned heavily on the local notable and lower scholar gentrymen (who at least shared their ruling-class language and culture) to govern as best they could. They were sometimes ignorant of, and more often helpless to prevent, recurrent abuses by the local notable and scholar gentry in the management of local affairs.

If they took their jobs seriously at all, China's lowest-level appointed officials, the county magistrates, had to be overworked men. In theory, at least, each was single-handedly responsible for all manner of executive, judicial, civil administrative, police, welfare, defense, educatonal, cultural, and ceremonial functions for an average population of perhaps 100,000 inhabitants.[44] As Jerome Grieder has so succinctly summarized the rationale for this arrangement:

It was the genius of the Confucian political system in this fashion to limit the range of imperial responsibilities—and the drain on the imperial treasury which the maintenance of a governmental structure that penetrated into every village and hamlet would have entailed—by delegating political functions at the local level to an elite not formally integrated into the governmental structure or supported at government expense. Thus it was that appointed officials all the way down to the level of district magistrate could act as the agents of the central authority, leaving it to local gentry both to implement imperial policy and, as the need arose and opportunity presented itself, to represent local interests. It was an arrangement, moreover, which had the entirely intentional effect of giving the gentry, in localities scattered across the broad territories of the empire, a greater concern for the well-being of the monarchical institution on which they depended for their status than for their own interests as a "class" or "estate."[45]

In fact, in addition to such local and scholar gentry assistance, each magistrate was obliged to gather round himself a somewhat motley corps of clerks and runners to handle the flow of official business. Secretaries, assistants, doormen, coroners, horsemen, jailers, grain measurers, guards, and lantern bearers could all commonly be found in the train of a county magistrate. As a rule, the salaries for such personnel were not amply provided for through treasury disbursements. Magistrates therefore often set aside a portion of their own allotments as retainers for each of these clerks and runners and expected them to supplement their incomes through the commonly tolerated practices of corruption, embezzlement, and the collection of "customary fees" or bribes. In all their official duties, county clerks and runners in turn relied on the local lower scholar gentry and village notable families for assistance, and most often became involved with them in one or another form of corruption. Since the very term 'corruption' is a pejorative one, let us see how Barrington Moore has tried to put the matter in perspective:

In any preindustrial society, the attempt to establish a large-scale bureaucracy soon runs into the difficulty that it is very hard to extract enough resources from the population to pay salaries and thereby make officials dependent on their superiors. The way in which the rulers try to get around this difficulty has a tremendous impact on the whole social structure. The French solution was the sale of offices, the Russian one, suitable to Russia's huge expanse of territory, was the granting of estates with serfs in return for service in tsarist officialdom. The Chinese solution was to permit more or less open corruption.[46]

Thus the county magistrates, their hireling clerks and runners, and the local educated and landed elite of the villages were all involved together in a conspiracy to get the work of the state done while making sure that all who helped were reimbursed for their services. With all the deductions attributable to gentry and official "corruption," total state collections were much less than in theory they should have been. But as Moore suggests, the difference represented the real cost of local governance under the actual conditions of imperial China.[47]

Tax collection provides the clearest examples. No doubt to induce their cooperation, gentry households were traditionally taxed at a lower rate than commoners'. There were, as Hsiao remarks, "two different categories of taxpayers," and gentry families enjoyed numerous tax privileges and immunities, such as exemption from labor services of all kinds.[48] Degreeholders often tried to get these privileges extended to ever-more-distant members of their families, and there was apparently constant haggling by the gentry over what rates should be applied to them. Historical accounts make it clear that in late imperial times the court and the bureaucracy were sometimes able to crack down on lower gentry transgressions, and sometimes not. By the late years of the Qing, however, one gathers the unmistakable impression that low-level officials were unable to curb local notable and scholar gentry tax evasion and the consequent overburdening of peasant households to meet local tax quotas:

As the local officials could not argue with the gentry on the legality of collecting extra surcharges or setting a higher conversion rate, they had to accept the lower rate paid by the gentry households in accordance with established usage, and meet the cost of collection and other yamen [district government] expenses covered by extra surcharges by shifting the burden onto the commoners, who were unable to protest and protect themselves under the law.[49]

Gentry tax evasion extended even to the assessments made on *other* families. Although it was illegal, local gentry often became tax farmers and acted as intermediaries between peasant taxpayers and county officials:[50]

The commoners sometimes sought this arrangement in order to avoid direct dealing with yamen personnel and their numerous techniques of extortion. The gentry stood to profit by collecting tax funds at the commoner-taxpayer's rate (a rate that included the customary extra surcharges) and paying to the government at the lower rate for gentry households, pocketing the difference.[51]

Or again:

In some localities yamen runners found it impossible to deal with powerful scholar-gentry defaulters. An imperial edict of 1818 . . . said that "bad scholars and big households of Ch'ao-yang and Chieh-yang (Kwangtung) assumed tax responsibilities for others and refused to pay taxes. In the worst cases, yamen agents dared not go to the village to urge payment." According to another source, taxpayers in Tung-kuan [Dongguan] (another district in the same province) often evaded payment of labor service imposts by putting themselves under the "protection" of "powerful villagers." The magistrate succumbed to the influence of the local gentry and made no attempt at adjusting tax burdens.[52]

Naturally such practices were hard to stamp out since everyone with an interest in the matter was served by the arrangement. The magistrate collected *some* taxes, perhaps as much as his corrupt runners would have delivered. The peasants avoided confronting the despised runners themselves and earned a little patronage from the local leading family. And the gentry, for their part, made a tidy sum in the turnover. Only the state lost.[53]

To summarize, then, the lowest-level state officials were indeed dependent on members of the nonofficial lower gentry for cooperation in such essential services as surplus extraction and the maintenance of social order. Because the state bureaucracy itself did not fully extend into the periphery, and the substitute yamen clerks and runners were notoriously (if understandably) self-serving, the official-nonofficial gentry relationship remained the crucial one. And because of their dependence on the lower gentry, county and district magistrates

found it difficult or impossible to intervene when gentry behavior and a defiant peasant community contravened the
mandates from above.

(b) *Roles primarily serving the gentry.* Yet when members of
the lower local notable or scholar gentry pursued self-interest
well beyond the normal, socially accepted limits, they entered
the category of *lieshen*, bad gentry, and they undermined even
the semblance of good local governance. Thus their depreda-
tions came to be recorded not only in popular stories and
folklore, but also in the pages of many an irate magistrate's
and censor's reports. "Bad gentry" beat up their tenants,
seized other people's land or public land, collected unlawful
fees, and levied their own private taxes. They sent armed
bands to harvest the crops of other farmers, they used the
local militia to make wanton arrests of their enemies, they
seized irrigation works and extorted money from peasants for
the purchase of "water certificates." [54] There is no need to detail the abuses here. Unchecked exploitation was quite widespread, especially perhaps in times of famine and other crises.
The muffled voices of the many who were oppressed speak
movingly from the pages of the assiduously compiled dynastic
records. But there was little relief forthcoming from the state.
Edicts and special laws were issued, to be sure, but Ch'u
concludes:

Despite these laws, the imperial government failed to prevent the gentry
from exploiting their privileged position and engaging in unlawful activities. The law leaving the responsibility of supervising them to the
local officials remained ineffective. In general these officials were not in a
position to control the gentry, especially those of superior status and
great influence. Moreover, normally the local officials had a tendency to
maintain friendly relations with the gentry, avoiding any offense to
them. [55]

The gentry-official synthesis was too valuable to be lost. Bar-
barism can almost always be redescribed as bad taste. Key
local relationships had to be preserved despite unsettling reports and embarrassing teahouse rumors. Life in the lower

hemisphere of the polity could be at least as brutal and un-forgiving of weakness as the "examination hell" of the bureaucrats and the imperial court intrigues of the eunuchs.

(c) *Roles primarily serving the community.* At the other extreme of local notable and scholar gentry behavior are their community service roles. Members of the gentry mediated village disputes, organized large-scale mutual aid arrangements, and underwrote festivals, theater troupes, and other recreational events. Sometimes they organized temple schools and relief granaries that could serve poorer villagers; but these were undependable. In many areas it was the gentry *not in office* who took the lead in promoting major water works or other development projects to benefit their localities. "Because their ties with their native places were permanent ones that engendered a sentimental attachment, the gentry seem to have felt that it was their responsibility to guard and promote the welfare of these communities. This sentiment was lacking among the magistrates and other local officials who were nonnatives."[56]

Thus, in good times, local gentrymen could be expected to "attempt to defend local interests against the encroachment of the government,"[57] and in worse times, their identification with the community could induce them to cooperate with, and even lead, local tax resistance movements. *In extremis,* the local notable and scholar gentry might even throw in their lot with "bandits" or incite the peasantry to armed uprisings against the state.[58]

They served the state as extensions of the bureaucracy's control in their localities. But that service was always hedged with many provisos. The gentry themselves often proved hard to control, even as their own influence over a locality and attachment to it were prone to become intense. Even when they were not in the thrall of localistic sentiment, they tended to conduct local affairs in a customarily corrupt complicity with yamen runners and magistrates that removed the realm of rural local governance from the rules and regulations of the official apparatus. It was a localistic, personalistic synthesis of bureaucratic and nonbureaucratic elements that served to make the processes of rural local governance sublimely impervious, at times, to central direction.

State Power in the Twentieth Century

By 1911, when the last of China's great dynasties finally folded itself into history, the old gentry coalition discussed here had been much altered by the severity of the nineteenth century's economic, demographic, and cultural strains on tradition.[59] The ancient compromise solutions to the problems of local governance were no longer available to Chinese leaders; but the problems very much remained for China to solve, lest they be "solved" for her by other powers. In the standard accounts of historians and eyewitnesses, the agonies of the Republican period that followed are generally explained in terms of both the economic and the political insolvency of the infant democracy: warlord strongholds, militarist cliques, party factions, and treasonous sellouts to foreign interests all figure in the *post hoc* diagnosis of the Republic's illegitimacy, of its institutional insufficiency, of the new state's impotence, both at the political center and in the village periphery. More recent research suggests a somewhat different appraisal, however, of that complex period from the final years of the Qing through the Republic. If the weakness at the center was never remedied during that interregnum, many impressive local efforts (both opportunistically and idealistically motivated) were made to establish new, viable economic and political institutions to respond to the rapidly evolving political economy. Some of those efforts drew on past Chinese tradition and precedent; others had a more foreign or more modern inspiration.[60] Several of them demonstrably left institutional, personnel, and infrastructural legacies that were later to serve the Communist Party handily in its reconstruction of the state.

The hypothesis that a residually cumulative statebuilding effort went on all through the Republican time of troubles is indeed worth pursuing. Certainly, even amid the chaos and corruption of the times, some new patterns of cohesive action were taking shape. (Indeed, given the desperate obsession of nearly all educated Chinese who lived through the May Fourth era with their national weakness and the humiliations of disorder, it would surely be strange if *none* of their sincere efforts had left a mark.) Yet, the fact remains that the Republican environment was profoundly unstable and hostile to economic and political institutionalization; its governments were not popularly anchored; and with the Japanese invasion and the social revolution that was brewing, even its more realistic and progressive reforms and institutions were going to be either radically remolded or swept away entirely.

Meanwhile the communists, struggling toward power from their base areas in the backward periphery, were developing ideas of their own about political representation, economic development, and the way to construct a strong state. They also had some useful Soviet models to mimic. Armed with rich experience and a vision of the future, after national reunification they were able to achieve an extraordinarily swift and powerful reassertion of central state presence and authority over social life. The normative orientations and the policies of the new party/state, backed up by force, actually redefined many key social units and social relationships, making certain units intolerable and certain groups outcasts, while absorbing the roles of other units and groups into the expanded sphere of the state itself. This was, to be sure, an activist, interventionist state on a scale never before achieved in China.

But the new party/state center *did not, could not,* and *plainly often did not wish to,* control everything. What it did control, it often controlled indirectly. It employed instruments ambivalently located between state and society, and the degree of self-conscious autonomy these instruments could display often confounded and enraged China's central planners (even if they disappointed some observers in the liberal-pluralist West). Within the new state's own bureaucratic apparatus, certain defenses arose against excessive central direction. And where the bureaucracy came face to face with less tractable, more coherent social units, such as the rural communities that are our focus here, new protective zones of local politics were prone to form. As in the zones of local politics associated with gentry governance, the proceedings and the people involved were influenced *partly* by central values and demands and *partly* by local norms and concerns. Under Mao the local governing roles and behaviors of postrevolutionary rural cadres—at team, brigade, and sometimes even commune levels—resembled (at least in some respects if, of course, not in all) those of the local lower gentry before them. Like the gentry, in complicity with low-level state officials these cadres tended to recreate zones of local politics, which once again, even under socialism, limited central state penetration and control of rural villages.

Pursuing further this direct comparison of local gentry and local cadre may help reveal certain problems and possibilities that were shared by the imperial and the Maoist states. It must be emphasized in advance, however, that Mao's cadres were not, in any simple sense, the lineal descendants of the gentry. Despite the allure of comparisons that *might* be made between certain strands of Confucian statecraft and certain elements of populism, anarchism, and agrarian idealism in Mao Thought, the causes of cadre-gentry behavioral similarities should not be sought in either conscious or unconscious memories of the imperial past. Other factors would have to enter such a comparative analysis, such as the vastness of the territory to be administered, the prevailing patterns of social organization in peasant villages, the smallness of the administrative group relative to the size of the rural population, and above all the *relative* restriction of advanced capitalist relations in the Maoist economy, as in the imperial economy. Contemporary structural factors like these—and not recollections of ancient theory and practice—would have to figure most importantly in any full-scale attempt at a *causal explanation* of the bureaucratic and behavioral similarities that are here but *tentatively described*.

Rural Cadre and Local Governance

The Chinese revolution and the agrarian reform movement that came with it radically remade the class structure of the countryside. In particular, land reform and subsequent collectivization brought about an enormous socioeconomic leveling, and quite a thorough elimination of the ethical, political, and property bases of the old gentry. But a new corps of leaders emerged from the now more homogenous countryside. Rural cadres, who started as young peasant fighters in the war against the Japanese and the Guomindang, or who emerged as audacious young activists in their local land reform struggle, were spotted and recruited by party members, cultivated, trained a little, and then thrust into the tasks of mass organization and local governance. They were chosen by the party to be cadres because they met certain requirements: they came from the right class background (mostly the poor and middle peasantry); they had the right attitude toward social reform; they were grateful to, and likely to comply with, the party; etc.

In other words, the status of rural cadre was something a peasant earned through personal talent and effort, but only with the approval of the new party/state. The cadre had to pass a test—many tests, actually—just as surely as the imperial examination system candidate. The state alone granted the rights and privileges of rural leadership, and in this sense cadres were heavily dependent on the state for the legitimacy, indeed the entire *raison d'être*, of their local rule. (Popular elections were held, of course, but only state-approved candidates could be in the race.) The party/state's rural cadres, like the gentry before them, were to embody the official state philosophy—now revolutionary socialism in the service of the poor peasantry. And their first duty was to live publicly in accord with those principles and to propagandize them among the people.

The new Chinese state depended on the rural cadres, as the old state had depended on the lower gentry, for the performance of such essential functions as surplus extraction and the maintenance of social order. Rural cadres were the vital lower links in the chain of agricultural tax collection, commodity quota deliveries to state procurement organs, and the administration of all other levies in the countryside. They also organized local militia units, and carried out mass struggle meetings, political campaigns, criticism/self-criticism sessions, home visits to remonstrate with recalcitrant scofflaws, and all other basic means of social control in the villages. Without the services of these cadres, for the most part recruited right from the localities where they worked and therefore familiar with special local conditions, local families, and local ways, the Communist Party leadership could not possibly have consolidated the new order so quickly throughout the vast peasant periphery.

Soon after liberation, however, two categories of rural cadres emerged. Some attained positions that put them on the state payroll; others remained members of collectives, remunerated in accord with their collective's fluctuating yearly receipts. With communization this distinction became sharply evident: commune-level cadres (and above) were on the state payroll; brigade (village) and team (hamlet) cadres were not. Thus, it seems, the Chinese state under socialism had indeed more deeply penetrated the countryside. After all, an administrative unit one level *below* the county (*xian*) was now indisputably staffed by officials paid directly by the state.

Nevertheless, certain qualifications are in order here. Even with the formation of people's communes, the county was the lowest level of rural administration to have a full complement of executive, judicial, and regulatory responsibilities. Communes, as a rule, employed a skeletal staff, and were by no means able to handle all aspects of rural local governance and welfare services. Counties, furthermore, were the lowest level of state administration to receive regular state budgetary allocations for their operations in addition to the allocations for cadre salaries.[61] Usually only a very small fraction of the working funds of a people's commune came from state finance channels. The commune was for the most part responsible for its own investments, profits, and losses. Thus, while their personal incomes came from the state, the working budgets and development ventures open to commune cadres almost entirely depended not on the state but on the fortunes of the commune-as-collective. At least some of the time, and in certain of their roles, therefore, this gave commune cadres a closer identification with their locality than is conveyed by depicting them simply as the lowest-level state officials. They were often caught somewhere in the middle, as this question-and-answer from an interview with a Guangdong commune cadre suggests:

Q: In carrying out the work of your unit, would you say you first thought about what upper levels wanted or first thought about the interest of your own commune?

A: The first thing we thought about was whether or not the peasants would accept it. If it was something the peasants could accept, then there was no problem; we could just go ahead with it. But if it was something that the peasants might not accept, or something they certainly would not accept, then it would be a lot of trouble for us. We'd have to find a way to take this policy and change it a little. Or else we'd have to find some other way to carry it out. Or we might even not carry it out at all.[62]

It was not uncommon for commune cadres to represent the views of "their" peasants to higher levels, to defend their localities against unpopular state rulings, and even to fail to execute prescribed policy to the letter in order to maintain the goodwill and cooperation of commune members. "Localist"

and paternal or protective behaviors were even more pronounced among team and brigade cadres, of course. Since
Dongguan county in Guangdong was cited in one of the accounts above as a place where peasants in the early nineteenth
century "put themselves under the protection" of local gentry
to evade state taxes and regulations, it is interesting to re-
count now some of the recollections of a cadre working in a
Dongguan county brigade supply and marketing coop (smc)
in the 1970s:

In our brigade smc we tended to try to handle problems that arose for
ourselves and did not expect help from higher levels or ask them for
help. We even did things that were illegal to solve our own problems.
One of these involved violation of the state's unified purchase and supply
policy. Adjacent to our commune was another commune called XX
commune and there they grew a lot of peanuts. But our commune grew
a lot of sugar cane. The land in our commune was not suitable for peanuts and the amount of oil supplied to us by the state did not meet our
needs. Now our brigade was very close to this other commune; our
people saw each other all the time and we were linked by marital ties. So
what happened? Our brigade party secretary and brigade leader and
several others in the brigade got their heads together to decide whether
or not it would be possible to trade some of our sugar for some of their
peanut oil. This [was] without a doubt illegal and not permissible. Both
of these commodities came under unified purchase and supply and both
should have been turned over to the state for distribution. At first the
party branch secretary didn't know what to do. He was a little afraid.
Then the brigade leader went over to consult with the people in XX
commune to see if they would agree. They replied that they'd be happy
to. They never had enough sugar you see. So a brigade boat was secretly
sent over there loaded with sugar and came back with peanut oil. We
didn't just do this once either; we did it many times. . . . No, we were
never found out by the commune; even other brigades didn't know
about it. Everybody in our brigade knew about it, of course, though.
No, the commune never sent anyone to our brigade to investigate this.
The commune so rarely sent people to investigate into brigade smc
affairs that this was one of the reasons our brigade cadres dared to try
this. Only if your smc was losing money did the commune send someone
to investigate. They might then suspect corruption or some other problem. But in our brigade, as I said before, we made money every month,
so they never sent anyone to check up.[63]

Or again:

Sometimes we did things without ever informing the commune smc too. For example, during the busy season the peasants didn't have time to take off to buy vegetables and other things to eat. So the brigade leader suggested that we could catch shrimp in the reservoir at night and have them ready for sale to brigade members in the morning. He discussed it with us and others first and then checked with the brigade party branch secretary, who also agreed that it was a good idea. On the one hand it meant we at the smc would earn a little more money. And on the other hand, it would be providing the brigade members with something better to eat. Of course, most of the shrimp and fish that we caught in the reservoir were supposed to be taken to the commune. So when we decided to do this during the busy season, we most certainly didn't tell the commune about it. . . . Yes, most everybody in the brigade knew about it and they knew it was illegal, but it was beneficial for them and so no one ever said anything to the commune cadres about it.[64]

Perhaps the commune cadres were in the dark about many such small transgressions. Sometimes, however, they must have winked at what they knew:

When the brigade smc purchased things, such as chickens, for the commune smc, they set a quota that we were supposed to meet. But as I told you, with the chickens, many peasants really didn't want to sell them to us because they could have gotten more for the chickens on the free market. So quite a few households would basically refuse to sell us the chickens. But it wouldn't do for us not to meet the quota. So what could we do? Well sometimes we told them that we had bought and paid for the chickens, but that some had died. Once we had a quota of 100 chickens to purchase. But we could only get 80. There was nothing to do but tell the commune that 20 had been purchased but had died. . . . But of course we couldn't stretch the story too far. It wouldn't work to claim that too many had just dropped dead. . . . There were a lot of little contradictions like this between us and the commune smc.[65]

Examples like these are very typical of the characterizations of rural cadre reasoning and behavior that could easily be gathered through émigré interviews in the 1970s.[66] The general picture that emerges is one of modulated but calculated localist protectionism by team and brigade leaders. As one informant summed up the behavior of a production team leader during investigative visits by higher-level cadres:

Was the team leader completely helpful to them in their investigations? Well I guess I really think he was sort of a useful tool for them. He wouldn't tell them everything exactly as it was. But he couldn't completely deceive them either. He wouldn't report everything for them to know, but he couldn't hide everything. But on economic matters— matters of team income—I think there *was* a little covering up, a little dishonesty. This was because if he reported too honestly on our income to the brigade, then the orders that would come down each year would be for us to turn over more to the brigade. And that would mean less income for the team members. So the team leader would just tell them what he had to; he wouldn't let them know the real situation.[67]

A few purloined shrimp, a little underestimation of the crop—it may be objected that these are but small protections and minimal decencies within a context overwhelmingly dominated by obedience to the state and its regulations. Just so. There is no assertion here that the peasantry under Mao was either blissfully content or even especially well-served by the policies and practices of the party/state. (Nor would it be an enviable task to try to make such an argument about the condition of the peasantry under the gentry and the imperial state, with which the comparison here is being made.) The point is simply that local cadres, like local gentry, could frequently make a difference *at the margins* for their people and their communities. It was not in their power to evade the greater part of the state's exactions, to be sure. But they could work to minimize local losses and to secure for their villages whatever small benefits the state had to offer, be it only a little more fertilizer or a little better schooling for the children. If their locality unfortunately ran afoul of some high official, was singled out for investigation, or became caught up in the whirlpool of a political campaign, then the local cadre could do little to deflect the heavy blows that *could* come from the fist of the party/state. But in normal times, if they kept their heads down and cultivated their ties to local officials, village cadres could glove the hand of state, dulling its senses as it probed into local affairs, and smoothing its stroke over the bent backs of the farmers.

Not all local cadres and officials played this game, of course. Those who did play did not always play consistently, or successfully. If political, careerist, or other personal considerations entered the picture, a local cadre might choose to behave like a model of obedience to the center, compromising if necessary the interests of his locality in the gambit. Rural cadres in the turbulent Maoist years certainly developed diverse motives and a varied repertoire of strategies and styles.[68] But it seems clear that most village cadres played some version of the local protectionist game enough of the time that it had the effect of pressing at least some local values, demands, and expectations upward into the bureaucracy, thus modifying the attitudes and behavior of lower-level officials and conditioning the norms and methods of policy implementation in the countryside.

From the point of view of rural officials who had to supervise the work of cadres below them, the secret to "getting along" within the system was not to ask too many challenging questions:

You know, even when higher levels come down and criticize cadres at the basic levels, they're uncomfortable doing it. They can of course criticize, if they are not satisfied with their work. Still, they depend on them to *do* the work, after all. If you curse them too much, it will be no use. Well, I mean, if you curse them *too* much it will have the opposite effect. If their work in the teams is too hard and they don't lead well, then the whole brigade will suffer, won't it? If you curse them too much, they won't have grain to sell to the state, and in the end won't that harm the whole brigade? So, enough is enough. On small questions anyway, they [brigade cadres] would rather overlook it and not cause a fuss with the team cadres.[69]

Thus, even at the period when the "ultra-left dictatorship" was supposed to have been at its most domineering apogee, rural cadres and officials at various levels routinely contrived to restrain central penetrations into their localities. Local affairs were handled more informally, more loosely, than state policy documents made it seem because, in the end, the official bureaucrats were dependent on the goodwill and voluntary assistance of local leaders who were not on the state payroll.[70]

As with rural gentry governance, however, the same zone of local politics that staved off state interference and superexploitation made it harder for the state to intervene to protect citizens when those who held power locally abused it. Every émigré informant who can describe the laudable local protectionism of a rural cadre also knows a story of cadre abuses. Repeatedly, over the entire period since 1949, Chinese Communist Party documents and press reports have scowled over continuing local cadre corruption, malfeasance, and bullying. Embezzlement, nepotism, vendettas against personal enemies, and sexual harassment of local women are all offenses very commonly cited. Redress of grievances like these is most difficult where political power, economic control, and social status all converge in a small, localized elite with numerous formal and informal ties to the state's official apparatus of control. Petty local despotism and petty local protectionism are two sides of the same coin in a peasant society that is not yet fully integrated into a modern polity penetrated by a modern state structure.

Rehearsing such realities of recent Chinese political life only reminds us that the social revolution in the villages did not automatically solve the problem of the administrative reach of the state. The real record of rural local governance in socialist China comes out rather far from the implicit expectations of even so shrewd a pioneer observer as Franz Schurmann, who wrote:

The Communists realized that [their] organization would have to be built up within the natural village, yet with assurance that it would be primarily loyal to the larger cause rather than to the narrower village interests. By creating a new Communist party and by training a new type of leader, the cadre, the Chinese Communists were finally able to achieve what no state power in Chinese history had been able to do: to create an organization loyal to the state which was also solidly imbedded in the natural village.[71]

Upon closer inspection it seems, China's "new type" of rural leaders did not represent such a dramatic break with the past. In many ways, at least, they perpetuated the contained but unrelenting central-local struggle characteristic of imperial politics.

Yet, might this be but a superficial similarity? Do not all complex organizations display some tension between the part and the whole; do not all state bureaucracies experience a certain degree of "leakage of authority" between center and locality? Is there, perhaps, something less in this cadre-gentry comparison than meets the eye?

Two aspects of the pattern of post-1949 rural local governance make the analogy with the multi-layered gentry and parcelized polity of China's imperial past especially worth preserving and pursuing. First, the Mao period saw a continued fusion of political authority, economic power, and social status in a small, highly integrated rural elite, which in turn made all its claims to authority from within the framework of a single, overarching moral and political value system. Second, the Mao period permitted only a very localized sphere of influence and authority to be exercised by any individual member of this rural elite. Under Mao, working within an administrative structure of nested territorial units, no rural cadre's influence network could extend very far without coming up against superior officials. This parcelized but complete power is what is so reminiscent of the old pattern of rural local governance. And today's reformers in Beijing have directly implicated certain policies of the Maoist era in perpetuating and exacerbating these seemingly paradoxical conditions of excessive domination and excessive fragmentation.

The policy known by the slogan "agriculture as the foundation" was one of these, as it was interpreted to give primary emphasis to raising output measured quantitatively, not in value terms. Each brigade and commune was encouraged to raise its own production of certain staple crops rather than to maximize the total value of its production through specialization and trade. Each unit hoarded production resources and cultivated beneficial horizontal linkages only at political risk. Handicrafts and consumer services were neglected in the effort to meet and exceed state-set targets for the production of staples. As a result, agricultural units turned inward upon themselves and became increasingly isolated from other units, socially as well as economically.

The policy of "self-reliance in agriculture and industrialization" was even more instrumental in isolating rural communities. Not only were communes and brigades to produce all their own basic consumption requirements, but, in attempting to bring some of the benefits of industry to their people, they were to draw only on raw materials and skills available locally, to set up low-technology workshops to produce low-quality goods to serve very restricted local markets. Official policy denigrated the rudimentary benefits of production in accord with comparative advantage, commercial exchange, shared technology, and subcontracting, in its preference for the ideal of local self-reliance.

The control of rural population mobility through the household registration system also helped segregate local economies into separate cells. Peasants were virtually tied to the land after the Great Leap Forward, and many local cadres became highly reluctant to allow their laborers to be utilized outside their own jurisdictions. As numerous villages vainly tried to cope with their growing surplus labor, commercial needs and service opportunities in neighboring units remained unmet.

All these features of the Maoist rural development strategy emphasized *locality* and severed or weakened any natural economic linkages between communities. Administrative practice followed suit, and the procedural significance and ethical standing of territorial boundaries hardened within the bureaucratic structure. All the while, local cadres were implored to think of themselves as "reds" first, and only secondarily as "experts." They were to avoid specialization of function, to retain an interest and an involvement in all aspects of local work. They were to be as omnicompetent, and as omniresponsible, as possible.

Thus the Maoist approach to rural development is now blamed for accentuating China's old but still incompletely transcended centrifugal and cellular tendencies. Seen from the perspective of any respectable centralizing statebuilder, party policies under Mao maddeningly abetted China's most ancient of political vices—the stubborn capacity to parcelize power locally, despite the best efforts of an integrating bureaucracy. Reform leaders of the 1980s argue that the heightened salience of *locality* in rural China under Mao inhibited efficient central direction of the economy, even as it exposed the hapless peasantry to the depradations of petty tyrants.

Just as China's old gentry, with its vested interests in the land, is associated with the *failure to make a decisive transition to industrial capitalism*, her latter-day local cadre elite is associated with the extreme anti-commercialism of ultra-left Maoism and thus the *failure to break through to a modernized economy under socialism*. According to the views of the Deng Xiaoping coalition, the take-off to industrialism will come via high-speed rural commercialization, which in turn will require the integration of formerly parcelized rural economic systems and the disaggregation of the formerly fused rural political, economic, and social elite. The breakthrough to a modern state and a modern economy as now envisioned in Beijing is going to require the breakdown of China's ancient, local protectionist, lower hemisphere of the polity. The values of growth through efficient interdependency—that is, the values of the modernizing state—are going to have to be driven all the way down to the bottom.

Modernization

Brief allusion was made in the initial preview of the argument to three reforms currently under way that are likely to have a profound effect on the pattern of rural local governance in China. In the context of the historical interpretation offered so far, it is hoped, we can now better understand the rationale, or the aspirations, behind these reforms.

(1) *Separation of powers in the people's communes.* By the end of 1984, at least on paper, *zhengshe fenkai*, separation of local civil government from cooperative economic activity, was carried out nationwide. Billed as a way of getting the state off the peasants' backs, the actual thrust of the reform seems more to break apart the fused economic and political leadership responsibilities of local cadres.[72] The social status of individual local leaders may become differentiated from their economic authority, which in turn will be distinguishable from their political roles. As for the economic activities of communes, now to be reorganized along the lines of companies and corporations, they are specifically encouraged to look outward for beneficial linkages with other units.[73] This reform attacks both the isolation of rural local economies and the fusion of powers of the local cadre elite.

(2) *Demarcation of new "economic zones" that administratively merge cities with surrounding rural counties and their communes.* The new zones will facilitate a freer exchange of resources and labor between urban and rural areas. This reform is billed as a way of removing state administrative barriers that inhibit rational flows of commerce and exchange. Integrated urban-rural zones are the antithesis of rural self-reliance, and when joined with the present emphasis on the need to develop more small towns and cities all over the country, this policy points to the eventual incorporation of all but the most remote villages into an urban-based pattern of economic growth. Indeed the present vision of modernization for China involves a vast "depeasantization" of the countryside,

the rapid shifting of people from primary reliance on cultivation into other occupations. Recent discussions in the Chinese media have predicted that in the coming decades as much as 70 percent of the current rural labor force will leave the land for jobs in the industrial and service sectors of the modernized economy.[74]

(3) *Upgrading the quality and technical skills of the rural cadre force.* The reform leaders want greater specialization and less overlapping of cadre functions. They want many cadres to be transformed into company executives who work for salary bonuses and are accountable to peasants and others through contractual agreements. The "red" jacks-of-all-trades, with personal prestige and influence but with little education, are to be replaced by more modern and efficient professionals. This "bureaucratic rationalizing" reform—admittedly one for the longer term—is billed as a way to relieve peasants of the burden of dead wood in the state apparatus.

With pointed reference to the dictatorial transgressions of the ultra-left, the Deng Xiaoping group thus promises the peasantry to pull the politicized state a few steps back out of village economic and social life. In the current atmosphere of greater tolerance for capitalist relations, higher procurement prices, greater labor mobility, and better rural incomes, most peasants may well chime in with their complaints against the old order and their support for the new. If the economy should take a turn for the worse, however, peasant support may become more tenuous. Either way, China's beleaguered peasants may, for the moment, choose to ignore what we in the West cannot—that there is no simple correlation between the development of a "free market" and the protection or empowerment of those who are poor and weak. Indeed, the burden of the history of capitalism's spread in the developing world must be to warn that the individual peasant family and its way of life can be as thoroughly dominated and destroyed by a stockholders' corporation as by a socialist dictatorship. However it comes about, "modernization" dissolves peasantries.

If all there is to choose, in the matter of modernization, is which form of destruction of the peasant way of life you prefer, then the uneven but real increases in the standard of living that a freer market has so far brought to China may well be worth the sacrifice of some of her already sullied principles of socialism. The pros and cons of a market economy must be argued elsewhere. They are not what is primarily at issue here, except insofar as the development of the market and capitalism are sometimes too glibly equated with the protection of the individual against the state. It is essential to recognize that more power to the market has not so far in human history, and does not now in China, *necessarily* mean less power for the state over society.

The passage from Max Weber quoted at the head of this essay reminds us that the process of modern statebuilding may occur under *either* capitalist *or* socialist relations of production. And indeed, when a relatively strong state power is already in existence—as in China now—the further development of capitalism has historically tended to lead not to lesser but to *greater* bureaucratic expansion and control. The fact that postrevolutionary China first experienced the second of the two scenarios entertained by Weber does *not* preclude further refinements of bureaucratic rule under conditions of expanded capitalist relations in the economy. Modernizing bureaucrats will no doubt seek to eliminate remaining "irrational" and "inefficient" zones of local politics that they suspect resist the values and requirements of modernism. However imperfectly those zones of local politics proved over the ages to reduce peasant vulnerability to outside powerholders, under Mao they were often all that stood between the peasantry and the twentieth century's trend toward statist dictatorship. Yet the viability of these protective zones is now in much greater peril from Deng's rationalizers and modernizers than it ever was from the cult of personality. The divine right monarchs, we might recall, claimed the authority to rule absolutely, dictatorially. But their true capacity to govern pales in comparison to that of any modern liberal state, no matter how bound up it may be in self-conscious checks and balances against usurpations of power, and no matter how scrupulous it may strive to be about protecting individual rights. With modernization, the pretensions of state power generally *do* become more bounded; but, by the same token, the social constructs impeding or diffusing the reach of the state also begin to weaken and dissolve. "Modern" states typically claim to know less; but they can do much more. This is but one of the melancholy ironies of what we sometimes call "political development."

For these reasons, at the very least, we should remain skeptical of the anti-statist banner under which the Deng group is pressing its reforms of the system of rural local governance. Clearly, the real targets of the Deng coalition's modernizing reforms are not central authority or bureaucratic control, but the unitary political, economic, and social authority of the local cadre elite and the relative self-containment of the economic units over which they presided. Their targets are precisely all those elements of the state structure and the state-society relationship under Mao that they believe had not fully transcended China's premodern history and social organization. And these are just the components of the rural local protectionist complicity that previously offered peasants their only defense against the worst excesses of state interference, the prerequisites for a zone of local politics not fully penetrated by central ambitions.

Under the current reforms, when peasants become "shareholders" in their communes-turned-corporations, and when, without the protections of a fully developed legal system, they go to sign contracts with corporation personnel, there is little reason to expect that they will actually have either more freedom or more influence than they have had in the past. The reverse seems rather more likely since now they will have to act as more isolated individuals trying to get the attention of detached technocrats. And without the supporting network of an organized community of peasants and cadres, it will almost certainly be harder to defy real pressure from above, when it comes.

If the roles of local cadres are now subdivided and rationalized and if parcelized economies are integrated into more modern, urban-based networks, certain checks against local tyranny may well be gained. But to whom will peasants turn for protection against unreasonable state and state-corporate exactions if these should perchance be proposed in future?

Some of the most recent evidence suggests that networks of personal ties and patronage may already be gaining strength precisely to fill the need for new forms of local protection in the countryside. But such groupings are purely utilitarian. They have no particular legal or ethical standing in the Chinese polity. Furthermore, such private networks can merely attenuate—they cannot adjudicate—the struggles between the relatively weak and the relatively strong that are to come.

To be sure, new forms of protection for the weak *with* ethical and legal standing *may* evolve, as they have in many of the advanced industrialized societies of the world. Yet what the experience of these societies teaches us is that the evolution of protective mechanisms that are even tolerably effective in the modern environment is tortuous and long; and change claims many casualties in the interim generations who are obliged to make their contributions to progress.

Some socialists, who have studied and admired the struggle of the Chinese peasantry in this century (and who are troubled by the implications of the recent reforms for the revolution that they made), now say that the problem the Chinese people will have to face is that Deng's reforms are too pragmatic and unprincipled. Yet this look back at China's past patterns of local governance, which sometimes served to limit the effective reach of the state, suggests that from the long-term perspective of the peasantry, the problem may prove to be not that the reforms are unprincipled, but that they are modern.

Four

Honeycomb and Web

The Process of Change in Rural China

Even though we may know why that which happened happened suddenly, we may still be in the dark about why it happened at all.
KARL POLANYI

*T*here was a sudden change of course in China when Mao died. On this, agreement is practically universal. Admittedly, looking on from the outside, we may have a tendency to over-rate the pace and thoroughness of the metamorphosis. Under Deng, as under Mao, official voices continue issuing inflated claims about the successes they have lately achieved in the ever-urgent effort to "transform" the economy, the environment, indeed the people, of China. Opposition and resistance to the policy changes of the Deng group—the deliberate, calculating sort as well as the sort that stem simply from habit—were widely evident in the early years after Mao's death. Nor have they yet quite vanished.[1] But even when such caveats as these are duly noted, the enormity of the shift that has taken place in a mere decade can hardly be missed.

Ten years ago one would have been thought lunatic to suggest that Chinese peasants would be urged by their government to abandon collective cultivation for family farming; that households short of labor power would be encouraged to hire their neighbors, and their neighbors' children, for seasonal wages; that richer peasants would be permitted to make private loans to poor friends at interest rates well above those charged at the bank and the credit coop; and that in the capital, Chinese finance and trade leaders would be engaged in consultations with Wall Street experts on the finer points of establishing and regulating markets for the exchange of securities and stocks.

Of course, we *do* know why what has happened happened so suddenly. Those who lead and support the power coalition in Beijing today include many of Mao Zedong's oldest and bitterest political enemies, and they are quite naturally *un*doing much of what they had long opposed in the Maoist political and economic program. The old helmsman himself predicted that just this would happen after he was gone; but even he may not have foreseen how little time it would take to bring it off. Only weeks after the funeral ceremonies came the seizure of power and the beginning of the massive campaign against ultra-leftism.[2] That was followed by months of maneuvering and negotiation, careful coalition building, and media-managed preparation of the public, so that by late 1978 the new policy program for the countryside could be clearly seen taking shape. Although unanimity within the ruling group will surely always elude the grasp of top leaders in a nation of China's complexity and hazardous position in the world, Deng Xiaoping (and those who helped him) must take considerable satisfaction in the skill with which the craft of high politics was practiced in those trying months when a new elite "consensus" had to be nurtured and a new national "mood" had to be pressed upon the people. And as for the Chinese people at large, they surely must admire and congratulate Deng and his friends for the civil peace which they managed, for the most part, to maintain through that dangerous transition.

So, after all, it was mostly a matter of elite "faction" struggle. The death of a legendary leader and some consummately skillful political work by the "opposition" survivors can go a long way toward explaining why it has all happened so quickly. And yet, might we still be "in the dark about why it happened at all"? What is "it," exactly, that has happened, anyway? Why is the current official line on "modernization," market reform, and political renovation the *one* on which consensus *could* be constructed in China after Mao? Why not some other variation of reform, more like that of the Soviets or some of the East European states? Why has the new ruling group in Beijing targeted some aspects of the Maoist political economy and *not* others? What, beyond mere political revenge and the desire to go down in history as more prescient than Mao himself, animates the reformers and informs their vision? And why, when headline after headline in the American press announces the advent of "capitalism" in Deng's China, do serious scholars take to the op-ed pages to correct such fatuous labeling and to point out how many aspects of the system we associate with the "Maoist" past survive comfortably and powerfully in the "reformist" present?[3]

To approach an understanding of what has been happening in the Chinese polity at this deeper level, we must look beyond the realm of elite power struggle and policy compromise. At crucial turning points, to be sure, that elevated sphere of public affairs plays its undeniably genuine, if only seemingly decisive, part in history. In the final analysis, however, it is but a thin stratum of intense activity poised atop a vast and slowly evolving polity, at once seeking to direct that polity and taking direction from it. To confine our investigations and theories of Chinese affairs to that realm would be akin to oceanographic research limited to studies of the creatures who inhabit the surface waters and measurements of the motion of the waves.

When we turn our eyes from the seething surface to the search for deeper processes—the search for the intricate interweaving of structures and forces that slowly shape the polity—we may discover as much continuity as change. Or, at the least, we may more readily observe and appreciate that which does not change overnight under a regime of "reform." We may find that the reformers share much, in their assumptions, programs, styles, and motives, with those (now excoriated) who preceded them. China's sea change under Deng may be breathtaking in its boldness and sweep. But it still derives its power and purpose from familiar underlying political forces, such as patriotism, imperial ambition, cultural anxiety, and national humiliation—forces that run many leagues deep in Chinese history.

What the Deng regime reformers share most plainly with their early Communist, Republican, and late-Qing predecessors is the determination to strengthen the nation. As they themselves might say, they are "modernizers," first and last. They feel not only pain and embarrassment at the poverty and backwardness that persisted under Mao; they regard these as grave threats to China's international security. In their view, the 1950s, '60s, and '70s may have seen some real gains in the domestic economy and social welfare, but these were grossly inadequate to the challenge China faced. The nation remained miserably poor and vulnerable. In that age of ICBMs, after all, what patriotic, thinking Chinese citizen could have seen the moldy doctrine of "people's war" as anything more than bluff and bluster? Maoism's official nostalgia for the guerrilla glories of the revolutionary era could scarcely have concealed the fact that Communist rule had brought China no closer to the superpower status that (surely!) was her natural geopolitical destiny.

Meanwhile, at home, the party/state of the late Mao era, though rhetorically bordering almost perpetually on dictatorial excess, must actually have looked increasingly frail and frustrated to the angry, out-of-power modernizers. The state may have operated a "planned" economy, but it was an economy that grew too slowly to aggrandize the state. Those modernizers holding state power now hope, by contrast, to preside over the fastest possible rate of economic development. And they believe that if they can keep the standard of living inching upward for most and soaring dramatically for some, they will have given the energetic Chinese people enough incentive to make them spend their days and nights working longer, harder, faster, and more efficiently. Political slogans and tactics may be adapted to assuage the sorest needs of the moment. State powerholders in the Deng era may even sound a call for "decentralization" of power and "limitations" on excessive state interference. But this should not be allowed to mislead us into thinking that their goals are in any deep sense "anti-statist." For their program stands, instead, squarely in China's long nationalist and state-strengthening tradition.

China's reform coalition of the 1980s may favor widening the role of the market in the economy, but this does not make its members "democrats" in their political inclinations.[4] They may want to harness once again the talents of China's bruised intellectuals for the protracted struggle to modernize science and technology, but that does not make them "liberals" aching for the free interplay of ideas.[5] They may decry the dead hand of bureaucracy and the insidiousness of corruption and favoritism in government, but that does not make them rampant "populists" out to overthrow established state authority. On the contrary, they are at least as much committed to the principle of a strong and sternly paternalist state, to guide the nation's pursuit of "wealth and power," as every Chinese political leader of stature has been for more than a century and a half. Mao, too, after all, had shared just that commitment to continuously renewing the vigor, the authority, and the revolutionary legitimacy of the party/state, so that it might continue confidently pointing the way to China's progress. His serious differences with the modernizers on this were always over means, not ends. (Perhaps that greater congruence of "statist" aims was one of the reasons he always opted to have his "rightist" enemies only purged, not poisoned.) But the modernizers in power in Beijing now believe that Mao's reckless means betrayed his avowed ends. He, and the ultra-leftists he patronized, did not succeed; they failed in their struggle to make the Chinese nation wealthy and powerful and the Chinese state strong and authoritative. Though today's modernizers will not by any means throw away all the legacy Mao has bequeathed them, they do believe they know a shorter and a surer route to *wealth* and *power*. The odds are, they are right on both counts.

What I have said so far about the relative failures of state power under Mao and the "statist" ambitions of the current leadership may be difficult to grasp in the midst of so much talk and speculation about market "freedoms" and "individual" responsibility emanating from China—especially with respect to trends in the countryside. The task that remains, then, is to lend some support to this preliminary analysis of the implications of the current situation, by tracing some of the deeper processes of structural and cultural evolution that have led up to it.

Plan of Discussion

First, I will try to indicate the main factors in the process by which a highly localized, highly segmented, cell-like pattern came to typify the organization of social and economic life in the Chinese countryside in the years following the revolution. This general form of organization is what I find it useful to call the *honeycomb* pattern of the polity under Mao. Then I will suggest how local officials and cadres, responding to the honeycomb structural environment on the one hand, and to the particular policies and political rhetoric emanating from the center on the other hand, devised an array of ploys and strategies that served in part to protect their localities against intrusive central demands while also enhancing their own administrative power and their own room for maneuver within the system. By the mid-1970s most of these local officials, I shall argue, had acquired such considerable leverage and such skill at evading or distorting central policy, that top leaders from whatever faction were greatly handicapped in getting *any* policy—even one that was generally beneficial— implemented widely *as it was intended to be implemented.* The lower levels of the state's apparatus, reflecting the parcelized or honeycomb socioeconomic structure over which it presided had, in fact, become a maze of power pockets and vested interests manned by people who were constrained to

mouth the rhetoric of revolution but who often had everything to gain by protecting and elaborating on the status quo.
Far from serving as robotic handmaidens of central domination, these stubborn, savvy, and often cynical local officials
came to constitute a formidable obstacle to real and effective
central penetration and control on the ground.

This analysis leads, in turn, to two important insights
about the probable motives and methods of the present reform leadership. *First,* as it was gathering power in the late
1970s, the Deng Xiaoping coalition certainly understood the
origins and nature of this serious obstacle to its *own* effective
rule in the countryside. And *second,* the wide-ranging rural
reform program it pursued was in part motivated by the new
leadership's determination to smash that very honeycomb pattern of economic organization, the entrenched power pockets,
and the conspiracies of misinformation that conditioned performance in the lower state apparatus.

Those old cell-like communities and bureaucratic units are
now being overridden by new systems and organizations that
deliberately transcend and link together small localities. They
are urged to spread and sprawl, free-form and *weblike,* as
they follow the "natural" networks of commercial exchange
between city and countryside. Small companies and corporate
business entities, scanning the horizon for opportunity and
profit, have been formed out of what before were inward-
looking and fairly self-sufficient brigades, communes, or counties. The threads of social intercourse are likewise stretching
beyond the local cell-wall boundaries of the recent past.

The situation is very fluid at present; the future, as always,
hard to predict. One thing, however, emerges fairly certainly
from this discussion. The ornate segmentation of power and
the localistic complicity among cadres and between cadres
and peasants that was characteristic of the honeycomb pattern of state-society interrelations in the past served as often
to deflect central penetrations as to assist them. Once we
understand this, the market-based weblike structural sub-

stitutes of the Deng reforms begin to seem rather porous, weak by comparison, and subject eventually, perhaps, to more efficient state (or state-corporate) penetration and direction than the close-weave loyalties and the defensive mechanisms of what had been an undercommercialized agricultural sector. In other words, the hypothesis offered is that all this seeming "liberal" market expansionism of the current leadership may yet serve a "statist" or "state-corporatist" *vision.*

Toward the Honeycomb: Trends in Rural Socioeconomic Structure under Mao

In the early 1950s, during the land reform campaign and the first stages of agricultural collectivization, some of the new party/state's policies and procedures in the countryside had the effect of accentuating the salience of the small locality— that is, the salience of the hamlet and the village—for the organization of peasant economic and social life. In the seizures of landlords' and rich peasants' property and the redistributions to tenants and poor peasants during the land reform campaign, for example, it was the *xiang* or village that was taken as the relevant unit. The size of the *xiang* has fluctuated widely, but then, on average, it contained fewer than a thousand people, living in four or five adjacent hamlets. Typically, three, four, or five *xiang* made up a periodic marketing area, focused on a one-street market town on the circuit of several itinerant peddlers but with only a few dark and grimy permanent shops, perhaps a lineage ancestral hall, and a teahouse.

The land reform programs of India and some other third world countries have frequently tried to set, if not a national, at least a statewide or regional minimum grant to all the landless and land poor—enough ideally to create viable family farms. In China, however, there were no long-distance transfers of land mediated by state offices and bureaus, and no regional standards. What a poor tenant family might receive depended entirely on just what there was to be divided up within its own village. If there were wealthy landlords to be expropriated, there was more. But if the best-off families in the village were just getting by, there was much less. The economic claims, the political rights, and, for that matter, the moral horizon of the Chinese peasant was assumed, from the earliest days of the People's Republic, not to stretch beyond the *xiang*.

At the same time, some of the designs followed by the young party/state in constituting and staffing its rural administrative apparatus abetted this tendency toward localist forms of organization. Village headships, for example, were not staffed by outsiders. On the contrary, activist youths who took the lead in the early revolutionary movements in the villages were deliberately recruited and drawn into the party to take up local leadership roles and offices. The party wanted, and made a concerted effort to get, personnel who were familiar with local history, local conditions, local families, and whose ties of sentiment would be likely to commit them to the welfare of the small community. Inevitably, a certain proportion of these young people, especially those with some literacy, would be promoted out of their villages to higher positions, perhaps as far up as the county government. But those who remained behind to lead in the villages were almost without exception local, mostly peasants, and parochial.

The boundary lines that separated peasant farming communities took on even greater clarity and significance during the early 1950s, as the linking and blending functions of itinerant peddlers and of the traditional periodic marketing networks were overridden by state trade monopolies in most major goods and commodities. With membership in mutual-aid teams and then farming collectives, the fates of individual, and formerly pretty independent, peasant households then became more and more intimately and absolutely linked to the welfare of their small communities. The homogenization of the village population that came with the leveling of land reform, and the increased interdependence of peasant households organized into the early collectives, each tended to thicken ties within hamlets and villages while dissolving ties to the outside.

With the formation of the people's communes during the Great Leap Forward, this process of imparting a marked pattern of rather discrete, cell-like units to the organization of rural life reached one of its impressive climaxes. The cells were larger now than the early collectives, encompassing usually at least a whole periodic marketing area. But this new creation, the commune, was explicitly conceived as a highly self-contained unit, in which economic life, social life, and political authority were fused in a single, comprehensive organization.[6] Internally, communes were to seek the increasing economic interdependence of their constituent teams and brigades, accumulating capital for investment from within their own borders, and working out a comprehensive plan for communal development. Externally, communes responded to production quotas and other demands sent down from county authorities, but they had little lateral intercourse with one another. The same principle applied to counties. They planned for the comprehensive development of their constituent communes and towns, but they had less and less intercourse with one another, as time went on often even erecting special tariffs and other trade barriers to imports from other counties. The honeycomb pattern was, by this time, already clearly emerging.

During the entire decade from the mid-1960s through the mid-1970s a series of radical, sometimes ultra-leftist, policies, articulated by shifting coalitions of central leaders in Beijing, served to accentuate even further the cellularity of communes and counties. The policy known by the slogan "take grain as the key link" was probably the most infamous of these. Grain-deficient rural production units were supposed to seek to produce enough staple grain for their own consumption, and those already self-sufficient in grain were supposed to strive to produce a surplus. Quantitative targets for sown area and for required sales to the state were issued by planning offices to press farming units into compliance. The targets were to be met even if it meant taking land and labor out of more lucrative cash crop and handicraft production. Peasants' private plots, where vegetables and sideline crops could be cultivated, also came under repeated attack because they competed with the collective grain fields for labor and time. The ideal of grain self-sufficiency for every commune may not initially have been intended to strangle rural markets, but it certainly had that effect. Peasant production and marketing outside the state-planned sector was reduced to a trickle, and all the various sorts of horizontal linkages between peasant communities that rested on the trellis of the rural free marketing network were further weakened. Opportunities for inter-village exchange of information were reduced and more restricted to officially sponsored occasions. Even local gossip networks tended to be circumscribed, and peasant communities became even more self-absorbed than before.

The principle of "self-reliance," when it was applied to the goal of industrializing and raising living standards in the countryside, yielded similarly isolating effects. Self-financed industrialization almost always meant that "appropriate" technology was low technology, raw material inputs were low-grade, product variety was limited, and product quality was unreliable. The markets served by rural industries built in the thrall of the "self-reliance" effort were usually highly localized and quickly saturated. But trade of all sorts with other units was to be avoided if possible. Subcontracting arrangements or other potentially more efficient divisions of labor and technical specialization were deliberately discouraged. The mentality of seeking to satisfy with local production the highest possible proportion of local needs became very strong among rural cadres. As late as the summer of 1979 I was told by a county commerce official in Hebei that before 1958, his office had to import from what he called "faraway cities" as much as 70 percent of the consumer goods sold in the county. But since 1958, he said with pride, about 80 percent of everything they sold to local residents came from within their own province.[7]

Meanwhile, the household registration system, in effect since the Great Leap Forward, made it virtually impossible for peasants to leave the land or to take up jobs in urban places. The horizons of their personal experience were delimited in proportion to the jealousy with which local cadres monopolized control over their labor. Elaborately negotiated agreements, with minute calculations of compensation, had to be made before a local official would agree to let even a handful of men go to another unit to do a job. It was not uncommon, in the 1970s, to be told by informants that in their villages there were many people who never traveled beyond the nearest one or two small market towns. The adolescent children of peasant families vied good-naturedly for the chance to be assigned to labor gangs going into the barren hills to do backbreaking work on water conservation projects. They had to make their own entertainment in the few hours between work's end and succumbing to sleep. But they looked forward just to getting out of the village and seeing something of the world and of other youths from other communes assigned to labor along with them.[8]

Many of these "leftist" policies, of course, held important advantages for China in meeting the larger challenges of development. Just to name a few of these advantages: the emphasis on grain quotas guaranteed the urban populations enough to eat; the state's trade monopolies prevented serious inflation; the restrictions on personal mobility saved China from the miseries of uncontrolled urbanization so visible elsewhere in Asia. To accomplish such ends as these, however, the honeycomb pattern of rural life was increasingly institutionalized, and the economic and social barriers separating rural communities were raised and reinforced. As just one more indication of the trend, sociologists noted that despite the long tradition of Chinese peasants marrying their daughters into households outside the natal village, it was becoming more and more common in the 1970s for matches to be arranged between young people from the same brigade or village.[9]

Politics: Strategies and Subcultures of Survival

So much for the main lines of structural change in the countryside. Meanwhile, another drama was being played out against this backdrop of socioeconomic segmentation and parcelization. China's rural local officials and cadres, working in the lowest reaches of the state bureaucracy—the counties, communes, brigades, and teams—rightly understood themselves to have been betrayed by the central leadership in the recriminations that followed the grievous setbacks of the Great Leap. These low-level functionaries were, in effect, made to take the blame and the public punishment for the squandering wastefulness that had come to the villages with utopianism, and for the agonies of famine and the austerities of the long recovery which remained to be endured when those utopian dreams turned into a national nightmare.

In its wilderness days, and in the early 1950s, the party had made much of its internal democracy and of the principle that ultimate responsibility for errors rested not with those who followed orders at the bottom, but with those at the very top who were supposed to be crafting policy and supervising implementation.[10] In 1959, however, faced with domestic economic chaos, with the increasing estrangement of the Soviet Union, and with the threatening posture of the U.S. Navy in the South China Sea, the shaken, angry, and mutually antagonistic groups at the center ended up sacrificing these basic party principles to sustain, instead, the *appearance* of order and unity and to maintain the *fiction* of yet another advance toward communism in the countryside.[11] The errors of the Great Leap were never, during Mao's lifetime, to be discussed and debated openly in China—not even *within* the party.

Central leaders never admitted their role in the sad fiasco. Instead, the message that clearly went forward was that the corruption and malfeasance of *local* cadres had been to blame for what went wrong in this village and that county. The "Four Cleanups" campaign, a vindictive purge aimed at local cadres and officials in the early 1960s, was to leave a wound in the polity that never properly healed.[12] Like all party rectification campaigns, this one was carried out by criticism and self-criticism, peer group accusations, struggle sessions, and confessions. Comrade turned on comrade, and this time it was no minor matter. A few were fined and suspended and made to suffer humiliation for what almost all had done together. In future, even among themselves, they would be much more circumspect on political questions. The lessons learned earlier by China's urban intellectuals in the "Hundred Flowers" campaign were now taught to her rural cadres. And as with the intellectuals, an outward veneer of obedience and enthusiasm came only thinly to disguise the underlying sense of abandonment and alienation of local officials, and to disguise not at all their swiftly developing ethic of self-preservation by any means.

With the onset of the Cultural Revolution in the mid-1960s, these local functionaries became enmeshed in a world of political discourse increasingly characterized by cant. Fear, accusation, public self-examination, and ritualized blametaking were the career minefields through which cadres at all levels trod to work each day. During the whole of this period, the factional struggle at the center kept it chronically weak— not, as some seem to have thought, domineeringly powerful. As it chattered its cheapened political rhetoric, scarcely comprehensible much less credible to ordinary people, it became an open secret that serving as a local official was a game of dodge-and-weave.[13]

As a general rule, most local officials clearly did what they could to resist state policies disadvantageous to their communities as long as possible, caving in if necessary under the concerted pressure of a campaign or under the probing eye of an investigatory workteam. Then they waited for the campaign to subside or for the workteam to go home, when they would quietly allow the *status quo ante* to be reinstated.[14] Given the extremely short attention span of central officials in those years of turbulent distractions, this alone was usually a pretty successful tactic.

But in the treacherous environment of that decade, many local cadres perfected even more elaborate and effective strategies for their own political survival *and* for the preservation and protection of their domains, the cellular communities of the countryside. Oversimplifying somewhat, it seems possible to discern *two broad types* of localistic cadre behavior that emerged in response to the structural and political environments of the late Mao era.

First, low-level officials became wily and dogged defenders of their localities, constantly resisting (as much as they dared), within the scope that was legitimately and not-so-legitimately available to them, the state's extractive designs on their particular corner of the countryside; and constantly seeking to *wrest* more allocations from state resources for their own locality in the general competition with neighboring localities. This was essentially a *defensive* strategy, involving concealment and misrepresentation of local conditions when reporting to superiors. The available scope for evasions and localist distortion of policy differed at different levels of the hierarchy, of course. The lower down, the less scope, and the more the ploys adopted were of this defensive sort.

At the team, the lowest level, according to informants who lived in the countryside during the 1970s, cadres were routinely able to protect their communities in the struggle with the state over the harvest, for example by simply underreporting output. (Most informants estimated that team cadres easily got away with anywhere from 5 to 15 percent off the top. All agreed that underreporting by 20 percent would have been pushing it too far and would probably have provoked an inspection by a workteam from the commune.)[15] Then also, team leaders helped peasants out by letting them raise a few more pigs than officially permitted, having the pigs slaughtered for feast days; by letting the threshing stop before all the grain was separated and dividing the still grain-laden chaff among the households; or, as in 1970, when the state restricted the size of community fishponds so that more land might be planted to grain, letting peasants dig out little ponds in their front yards—and so on.

Although the scope of action here was limited, the complicity of these cadres with peasants trying to evade state demands often clearly showed their commitment to a set of values at odds with those expressed at higher levels of the party/state. Each act of community protectionism was an expression of silent dissent from the "class struggle" ideology and from the moral primacy of the goal of state-guided national economic growth articulated, without respite, by central authorities. Their actions in defense of the peasantry were rooted in an alternative morality, indeed an alternative culture, to the one promoted by the state-socialist center. These cadres at the very bottom often also enjoyed a freedom to speak out and bargain openly with higher levels that went beyond what cadres at superior levels, more vulnerable to politics, would have dared. To quote one informant:

The teams all operated according to a plan [made at higher levels] that called for yearly increases in output. For example, the plan might call for the team to open a certain amount of uncultivated land that was still available, and it would include an estimate of the size of the land and how much it could be expected to produce once it was opened. It was in this kind of case that the peasants would argue for a lower quota. They'd say, "How can you possibly estimate that to be twenty *mou*? It'll only be ten *mou* of new land when we get done." Or they'd say, "How can you figure that land to produce 500 catties per *mou*? We'll only get 300. You know perfectly well new land never has that high an output." And so on and so forth like that. So, in this way they would argue back and forth about it (*zhenglai zhengqu*). And in the end they'd get the figure revised downward somewhat. Yes, this sort of thing happened all the time. . . . In other words, it was sort of like going to the market to buy something and bargaining for it. The brigade would bargain with the commune (*taojia huanjia taojia huanjia*) to get their quota reduced a little. And the team and brigade would bargain [with each other] like this too.[16]

Higher up, at the commune level, conflict tended to be less overt, but the scope for evading rules and regulations was often much greater. One cadre working in a commune special unit frequently selected as a model unit and one where almost everyone was a party or youth league member reported:

Basically, on crucial matters (*guanjian de wentishang*) they [at the county] had no way to supervise (*jiandu*) us. On financial matters and on matters of production discipline they really had no way of supervising our work closely. . . . It was very easy to hide things from the higher levels. . . . Sometimes also we [even] broke state laws. Once our unit said it was sending a man outside to purchase materials needed for production. But in reality that's not what he was doing. He went to XX county to buy some lumber at the free market there and to bring it back. Lumber is a special product of XX county. Now he bought this lumber really cheap. But when we got it back to our commune, we sold it to the peasants for a much higher price. In reality this was a kind of speculation (*tou ji daoba*), and we just called it by another name. Lumber was very scarce in our county, and extremely expensive. One cubit of lumber cost more than 90 *kuai*; but we bought it in XX county for a little over 60 *kuai*. We sold it to the peasants in the commune though for between 70 and 80 *kuai*. Of course they were very happy to be able to buy the wood from us. So we did this sort of thing to earn money [and helped them out too]. Yes, we trucked the lumber from XX county to Guangzhou and had it tied into bundles there, and then we asked some fishermen to transport it to our commune. Oh yes, this was illegal! No, we weren't caught. It would be very hard for them to find out, because the man who did this was carrying commune documents saying he was going to do some purchasing for us. There was no way for the county to find out about it. And even if sometimes they knew about it, they had no way to stop it. . . . You see, at the county there were also cadres who did this sort of thing. In fact the county sent some men to the Northeast to buy steel. They went to Wuhan and Qinghai, or was it Baodou? They were also really engaged in illegal speculation. When they got the stuff back to our county they sold it to us for a high price. So, in a way, they were hardly able to complain about what *we* were doing.[17]

At the commune and county levels, the scope for localist resistance to state demands was wider, but the fear of being the target of a political campaign was also greater, and therefore there was little *open* opposition or bargaining of the sort that peasants and team cadres could conduct. County cadres, however, understood well that just because their plans and demands elicited little explicit opposition from commune officials, that did not mean that everyone below was going to fall in line. As one young county cadre explained:

You've got to realize that the commune secretary is also a state cadre. He gets his salary from the state. If he opposes the plan of the county committee, then he risks making a bad impression. So in order to protect their own positions, even if they had objections in their hearts, most of them would on the surface appear to accept the county's plans. . . . But a plan is just a plan. When the autumn harvest came we'd see what they did in grain production. If they were able to meet the target, then that was good. And if they didn't, no questions were asked. . . . They'd give their reasons, why they couldn't achieve 100 percent, and if they made 80 percent say, that would be okay. It could even be a worse showing than that, and if they had good reasons, they would not be criticized or punished. This way of doing things is the experience, or the expertise, that goes with being a cadre. If you always do things this way, then you can succeed within the organization. If on the other hand, every time a little problem comes up you rush off to oppose the higher levels, then very quickly you will find you have lost your position.[18]

This fellow summed it all up with an ironic flair when he told me:

The plans [we made at the county for each of the communes to follow] departed from reality not by an *enormous* amount, but by a little. You see, this was the time of Lin Biao and the Gang of Four; it was a time of ultra-left policy. *Many* things at that time departed from reality. We all knew this. . . . You see in China we really do have a lot of experience in politics.[19]

The *second* of the two broad types of localist behavior among cadres was less defensive, more bold in the tactics adopted, and more aggressive in the aims pursued. This type of behavior tended to be concentrated at the higher levels of commune and county, but there are numerous accounts of it to be found down in the brigades as well. "Localist" or, as they were sometimes called, "departmentalist" cadres in this category specialized in learning how to use the leftist policies of the center to serve their own ends. These cadres did not merely evade, dissemble, or feign ineptitude to shield their units from central dictates and demands. They deliberately dug in their heels during tough negotiations with superior officials on matters that affected local welfare and development. With a rather "entrepreneurial" eye, they calculated how to bend the rules of the state-planned economy and stretch the guidelines of state-managed finance, gradually turning themselves into "socialist wheeler-dealers" who manipulated people and possibilities to serve local interests even as they were *enhancing their own power* within the system. Their goal most often was to accumulate resources, at their own level of administration or under the purview of their own office or department, for the construction of what they hoped would become independent local economic bases under their own control. If they succeeded, they hoped these diminutive economic empires would give them a position of some strength from which to continue to negotiate with their superiors for further concessions and preferential treatment that would ultimately serve the locality's overall development.[20]

All this busy opportunism on the part of local cadres made its contribution to the general trend toward dispersion of economic power downward through the system in these years. During the late 1960s and throughout the 1970s, as recent research has shown, decisionmaking authority and economic control were moving away from the center and coalescing in the provinces and the localities.[21] In a north China county, during a 1979 series of interviews with county officials on local government and economy, the implications of this trend emerged very clearly. In 1959, county finance officials reported, of all monies spent in the county, only 1.2 percent were funds over which county-level officials themselves had complete discretion. All the rest was budgeted very closely in consultation with finance officials at higher levels of government. By 1977, however, thanks mostly to the principle of self-reliant industrialization, which had allowed the county to build several small but profitable factories whose earnings county cadres themselves had negotiated to control, over 30 percent of all monies expended there were funds over which the county alone had discretion. They spent those funds locally, as they saw fit. And often their preferences interfered with the state plan. At the very least, this arrangement prevented the center getting its hands on those monies for possible redistribution to other areas.[22]

The same pattern of accumulation of economic clout in the province, the county, and the commune can be found to have emerged all over China in the 1970s. In agriculturally rich and developmentally promising areas such as Guangdong and Jiangsu, the phenomenon often extended down even a step further, to the brigade level. In comparatively wealthy areas like those, even agricultural production brigades were often financially able to establish small but lucrative enterprises, workshops, and factories under their own jurisdiction and control. In accord with the "leftist" principles of promoting local self-reliance and rural self-industrialization, such small "collective" enterprises received significant tax breaks and other incentives to get their business under way. Brigade cadres, in turn, deliberately made use of these policies to earn income for their own units, and to get control for themselves over the profits, the products, and the other resources of these enterprises. Their authority and discretion in making investment and distribution decisions steadily grew. But their plans and preferences did not by any means always coincide with those of the central planners. Thus, the financial and planning control the center was losing to the localities it may have been losing most decisively in the wealthier parts of the country, where it might have stood to gain the most through economic growth.[23]

The ultra-left rhetoric of those years frightened almost everyone, and it is apparent that local bureaucrats and cadres were allowing the ideologues to win many *political* battles by default. But it also seems very clear that the self-flagellating state center was not winning the larger *economic* war. By the mid-1970s, almost every economic reform and policy initiative announced at the center had to be negotiated and compromised somewhat to meet the stubborn demands of local officials, who were increasingly in a position to affect economic outcomes. The picture of the countryside projected by the central leadership, featuring social consensus and generous sacrifice for the national interest, was very far indeed from the real worlds of shrewd and wary peasant cadres trying to con the state, and competitive, calculating local politicos fighting over turf.

It must be added that each of these behaviors—cadre responses to the structural and political environment that were originally justified in the localist morality of community—was prone to deep distortion and corruption. And in their corrupted forms, these behavior patterns crossed the border into personal immorality and sheer exploitation. Cadres practicing defensive and dissembling strategies needed to be good at maintaining networks of allies and associates who would assist them in concealing the truth. They often naturally turned first to trusted relatives and friends, and they were inclined to see to it that these people received appointments to key positions in the local power elite. Controlling as they did all access to the few special privileges and opportunities that were available to rural people, they made sure their families and favorites got first crack at coveted places in middle school or at recruitment into the army.

Nepotism and petty favoritism have a long, and not always dishonorable, pedigree as part of China's political culture. In fact, it can be argued that part of the dilemma these local cadres faced was that *not* to favor one's familiy or lineage once in power would have been widely regarded as unfeeling, inhuman, or possibly even immoral, in the Chinese context.[24] But it is a characteristic of complex moral questions in all societies that what one "ought" to do is usually not an "either/or" question, but a question of degree. How far can one go in favoring one's family with political appointments before one has gone *too* far? That was usually the actual question the team, brigade, and commune cadres had to face. And there is little doubt that, even in the eyes of rural people who shared the familist morality, many local cadres did go too far, and thus became corrupt. For those villagers who were not on the local cadres' list of favorites, real daily privations and the apparent hopelessness of ever securing better life-chances for their children surely made their experience of the localist system profoundly frustrating and bitterly unfair. The cellular polity, with its general imperviousness to thorough central fact-finding investigations and with the latitude it allowed local cadre bosses, often left spaces where quite venal village despotisms could be perpetrated (and perpetuated for many years) with impunity.

Cadres pursuing the more aggressive localist strategies found that they, too, could fall into moral traps that lost them the support of their peasant constituents. "Socialist wheeler-dealers," trying to maximize their influence and their control of resources, frequently felt themselves under pressure to get rapid results. They were tempted, therefore, to impose exactions and demands on local people in support of their own pet projects, whether or not these people were genuinely persuaded to go along. County, commune, and brigade cadres of this "entrepreneurial" cast of mind squeezed labor and other contributions out of subordinate units, and simply appropriated material they wanted, promising airily that some day it would all be given back, and more. Projects collapsed, enterprises floundered, debts were not repaid, and these cadres too earned the enmity of the peasants and the title of "local tyrants."

In constructing their wholesale critique of the Maoist past and its "crimes," Deng's allies have found it useful to emphasize and exaggerate these patterns of local cadre corruption and immorality. In the wake of this devastating official reevaluation of recent history, outside observers may never find ways of discovering just how widespread truly "corrupted"

forms of localist behavior became in comparison to those cadre strategies that managed to remain rooted in the popular
morality of community protectionism. We certainly cannot
dismiss the charges of corruption and tyranny as mere in-
ventions of the political opposition. At best we can try to trace
their tangled roots in the processes of social-structural evolution and in the repertoire of available cultural responses that
characterized the times.

The Webs of Commerce

As the two previous sections have endeavored to show, the
honeycomb polity under Mao, along with its special strengths
and weaknesses, was the product of a lengthy process of mutually conditioning interactions between evolving social structure on the one hand, and changing political and cultural op-
tions on the other. The increasingly parcelized socioeconomic
structure, *plus* the particular experiences and mindsets of the
cadres who manned that structure, *plus* the high-pressure
politics of fear of the Cultural Revolution era produced a variety of defensively and aggressively localistic strategies in the
lower bureaucracy, along with a general ethic of not giving full
information to superiors while winking at the violations and
transgressions of subordinates. It was this conjuncture in the
1970s of ongoing structural trends, shifting political forces,
and eroding attitudes and behavioral norms that made the
everyday work of Chinese government and politics such a peculiarly unsettled mix of intensity and lethargy, activism and
paralysis.

Even so, is it really useful to speak loosely, as I have done
here, of the "failures" of state power and of the "weakness"
of the Chinese state in the late Mao era? A more accurate formulation would probably be that by the 1970s, at least in the
countryside, state power had been not so much weakened as
deeply compromised and fettered by the forces of localism.
When Gulliver awoke on the shores of Lilliput, his muscles

and sinews had not lost their strength. Yet he found himself unable to move, tied down as he was by numberless tiny strands, each in itself a scarcely noticeable impediment. Fettered by the fearful (but cunning and industrious) Lilliputians, Gulliver writhed and bellowed; but he could not rise. Similarly, I would suggest, the Chinese state center through the 1970s remained full of force and loud intention, but was nonetheless deeply frustrated in execution by thousands upon thousands of practically invisible localist restraints.

It is precisely this frustration, this immobilism, this insidious adaptation of primordial peasant localism to the honeycomb structure of the state-socialist polity that the modernizing leaders of the 1980s are out to overcome. The Deng coalition reformers have also apparently understood that, to overcome this daunting obstacle to effective state action in China today, they must attack *both* the old cellular structure of rural life *and* the subcultures of localism (both honest and corrupt) that thrived in its recesses. For this double attack, however, they have employed but a single weapon—rapid expansion of the role of market relations in economy, society, and the very work of local government. With this one weapon they have shaken both the organizational skeleton of the honeycomb polity and the morality of localism that both legitimized and stiffened it.

Collectivization has been undone. The basic farming unit is now, once again, the peasant household. This fact alone has worked powerfully to reduce the salience of the village community as a central unit of social life. The deliberate commodification of the rural economy has also quickly spun new networks of social relations that successfully extend the horizons of peasants and cadres well beyond the old cellular community units of the past. Internally, rural villages are becoming less socially homogenous, and therefore less solidary; externally, they are swiftly being enmeshed in the spreading webs of commerce. Communes (and even whole counties) are being reorganized into companies and corporation-like conglomerates that operate for profit and deal with all suppliers and customers, including organs of the state, through contractual rather than hierarchical command relationships. The formerly integrated powers of low-level cadres over almost all local social, economic, and political affairs are being broken down and separated out in the effort to get these people working more like corporate executives and technical specialists than like local patriarchs and politicians. Rural cadres with economic responsibilities are now urged to look beyond their own localities for opportunity and for new units and networks with which to identify and cooperate in seeking mutual benefit.

In the contemporary village-state relationship, both sides are undergoing profound structural and normative change. While village communities may be losing some of their internal coherence and their old corporate peasant identities and values, the party/state bureaucracy is busy reorganizing itself and putting itself forward in a more pleasing form. Local cadres are donning the trappings of "staff members" and "technicians" who work for combined collective and government-backed enterprises that operate for profit while they facilitate commerce and trade for farmers. In many places peasants themselves are also being turned into part-time employees and shareholders in the local corporation. And insofar as they operate in the marketized sector of the economy, these cadre/businessmen appear to act as independents, once removed from direct service to the state and the state plan.

Yet if current ambitious national development plans are to be achieved, these new state-corporate entities will have to become even better at generating and extracting resources from agriculture for national investment in industry and basic infrastructure. These new-style officials may be supposed to act more like independent entrepreneurs now. But their real status is highly ambivalent and their "stateness" may not have changed all that much. Their responsibilities to the offices of state, which still choose either to back or not to back their business undertakings with credit, contracts, grants, and licenses, are less direct now, but they may not be less absolute. Plainly, the reform coalition reasons that indirect levers like tax breaks and credit policy can often get better results than direct state controls over production quotas and prices. Indirect guidance through judicious manipulation of certain marketlike mechanisms may work better than direct bureaucratic commands to press the economy forward to desired performance levels. But whether it is direct commands or indirect levers that are employed, the principle that state leaders, ministerial development experts, provincial planners, central bank officials, and the like should be plotting the goals and guidelines as well as reaping the rewards of revenue and reinvestment is not in dispute.

How we should actually be conceiving of the new Chinese "state formation" now is uncertain, I believe. All these intriguing new state-corporate contrivances may be playing an important role in enlivening the rural economy; but do they not remain tethered to one or another level of government? And in the crunch, could they still be made to operate primarily as instruments of state, even within an economic framework that allowed more of a role for "the market"? Perhaps, and perhaps not. Despite some obvious temptations to try to reassert stern government controls, it may be that China's genie of expanding market relations has already grown much too hefty to be stuffed back into its bottle by means of a simple political crackdown of the old sort. The evidence mounts daily that new, growing, and potentially very powerful economic elites are emerging in the Chinese countryside. Their roles will be crucial. Yet, so far the nature, the strength, and the variety of their structural linkages to organs of state, as well as their personal ties to members of the state apparatus, remain untested and in doubt.

What are the terms of coexistence and cooperation that will be worked out between these new economic elites and the (also changing) local government elites in rural areas? And will the terms of their new alliances tend to reduce—or to enhance—the power and authority of the state in rural life? The range of possibilities for new forms of competition and accommodation between local government personnel and the rising economic elites in the countryside now appears open-ended, to say the least.[25] The two elites may become fully merged, with influential individuals generally holding both governmental offices and (collective or private) economic power and position. Alternatively, the two elite hierarchies may remain more distinct but achieve cooperation through illicit collusion or mutual cooptation by means of bribery, extortion, or other kinds of pressures and deals. Still again, the two elites may seek a kind of peaceful coexistence, in which separate spheres of influence remain clearly outlined, but agreed-upon groundrules guide and contain various forms of potential competition between them. Or finally, the two local elites may fail to find sufficient common interest to avoid open and recurrent conflict.

The situation in the Chinese countryside is in such flux now, and conditions vary so greatly from locality to locality, that it is not difficult to find some evidence that each of these patterns is already taking shape. Whether there will be a unified solution, or some patchwork combination of the possibilities listed above, is simply not yet known. The process which led to the earlier crystallization of the honeycomb pattern was, after all, long, multi-faceted, uneven, and complex. We should expect no less for the remolding of the Chinese political economy that is now under way. In the final analysis, we will probably want to avoid posing our questions in terms so simple as whether the state, on balance, gets "stronger" or "weaker" as a consequence of the post-Mao reforms. Such questions imply a kind of gross zero-sum competition between state and society which clearly misses the mutually conditioning interplay of structures and forces that these four essays have aimed to highlight. In that final analysis, we will choose instead to ask questions about how the forms and ethos of the state were altered; how the structure and ideals of society evolved; and how, in consequence, state-society conflicts, interpenetrations, and alliances were remolded. But for now, standing amid the confusions of a historical turning point, gazing backward at the honeycomb polity under Mao and forward into Deng's webs of commerce, we may perhaps allow ourselves a few broad speculations about the future.

If the new local economic and governmental elites referred to above do successfully negotiate this period of transition and find formulas for working in tandem, the resulting new state-corporate power structure in the countryside could well prove a good deal more efficient, as well as more wholeheartedly responsive to the visions of modernization and development emanating from the national leadership, than were the wary localist cadres of the Maoist past. In light of what we know about the processes of rural change in past decades, it is clear that in China political "reform" can have the most ironic of consequences. And in light of what we know about the processes of "modernization" in Asia generally, we certainly cannot assume that systemic "reforms," pursued primarily to attain economic efficiency and administrative rationalization, will necessarily bring with them enhanced political influence or democratic freedoms for the masses of rural people. What we may find ourselves witnessing over the next several decades, therefore, under the rubric of liberalization and reform of the excessively dictatorial state-socialist bureaucracy, may not in fact be the retreat of the state from stringent rule over the peasantry, but the rerooting of a relegitimized and reinvigorated state power in new social groups, and the reorganization, restaffing, and reconsolidation of the state apparatus itself in new, more effective forms. These forms may well be better designed than were the honeycomb patterns of the Mao era to achieve that long-cherished goal of China's twentieth-century rulers—full-speed, state-guided, nationalist and socialist modernization.

Notes

Notes

Introduction

1. The *locus classicus* is G. William Skinner, "Marketing and Social Structure in Rural China," Parts I–III, *Journal of Asian Studies*, Vol. 24, 1964–65. See also G. William Skinner, "Chinese Peasants and the Closed Community: An Open and Shut Case," *Comparative Studies in Society and History*, Vol. 13, No. 3 (Jul 1971):270–81.

2. Audrey Donnithorne, "China's Cellular Economy: Some Economic Trends Since the Cultural Revolution," *China Quarterly*, No. 52 (1972):605–19.

3. Nicholas R. Lardy, "Centralization and Decentralization in China's Fiscal Management," *China Quarterly*, No. 61 (1975):25–60.

Chapter One

1. Outstanding among the exceptions for the 1960s was Franz Schurmann's *Ideology and Organization in Communist China* (Berkeley: University of California Press, 1966), which, except for the curious omission of "the army" (see p. 12), stands as the pioneering study of both state structure and state links to various units of social organization under Mao. Notable for the 1970s perhaps, were the thoughtful efforts of the several contributors to Victor Nee and David Mozingo, eds., *State and Society in Contemporary China* (Ithaca, N.Y.: Cornell University Press, 1983). Although not published until well into the Deng era, this volume grew out of a workshop held in the spring of 1978.

2. Just a few of the influential and very varied works in this group would include: William Hinton, *Fanshen* (New York: Vintage Books, 1966); James R. Townsend, *Political Participation in Communist China* (Berkeley: University of California Press, 1967); Benjamin Schwartz, *Communism and China: Ideology in Flux* (Cambridge, Mass.: Harvard University Press, 1968); Maurice Meisner, "Utopian Goals and Ascetic Values in Chinese Communist Ideology," *Journal of Asian Studies,* Vol.

28, No. 1 (1968); Stuart Schram, "The Party in Chinese Communist Ideology," *China Quarterly*, No. 38 (Apr–Jun 1969); Maurice Meisner, "Leninism and Maoism: Some Populist Perspectives on Marxism-Leninism," *China Quarterly*, No. 45 (1971); Stuart Schram, "Mao Tsetung and the Theory of the Permanent Revolution," *China Quarterly*, No. 46 (Apr–Jun 1971); Mark Selden, *The Yenan Way in Revolutionary China* (Cambridge, Mass.: Harvard University Press, 1971); Richard Pfeffer, "Serving the People and Continuing the Revolution," *China Quarterly*, No. 52 (Oct–Dec 1972):620–53; Frederic Wakeman, *History and Will* (Berkeley: University of California Press, 1973); most of the essays in Stuart Schram, ed., *Authority, Participation and Cultural Change in China* (Cambridge, Eng.: Cambridge University Press, 1973); John Bryan Starr, *Ideology and Culture: An Introduction to the Dialectic of Contemporary Chinese Politics* (New York: Harper & Row, 1973); Richard Solomon, "From Commitment to Cant: The Evolving Functions of Ideology in the Revolutionary Process," in Chalmers Johnson, ed., *Ideology and Politics in Contemporary China* (Seattle: University of Washington Press, 1973); Mitch Meisner, "Ideology and Consciousness in Chinese Material Development," *Politics and Society*, Vol. 5, No. 1 (1975); and John Bryan Starr, *Continuing the Revolution: The Political Thought of Mao* (Princeton, N.J.: Princeton University Press, 1979).

3. Echoes of this approach can also be found in Gordon White, "The Postrevolutionary State," in Victor Nee and David Mozingo, eds., *State and Society in Contemporary China*, esp. pp. 33–34.

4. E.g., the classic work by A. Doak Barnett, *Cadres, Bureaucracy, and Political Power in Communist China* (New York: Columbia University Press, 1967); and the influential essay by Parris H. Chang, "Research Notes on the Changing Loci of Decision in the CCP," *China Quarterly*, No. 44 (Sep–Dec 1970):181–94. See also several works employing an "arena approach" to Chinese policymaking: Michel Oksenberg, "The Chinese Policy Process and the Public Health Issue: An Arena Approach," *Studies in Comparative Communism*, Vol. 7, No. 4 (1974):375–408; and David M. Lampton, "Policy Arenas and the Study of Chinese Politics," *Studies in Comparative Communism*, Vol. 7, No. 4 (1974):409–13; also David M. Lampton, *Health, Conflict, and the Chinese Political System* (Ann Arbor: Center for Chinese Studies, University of Michigan, 1974).

5. E.g., Michel Oksenberg, "Getting Ahead and Along in Communist China: The Ladder of Success on the Eve of the Cultural Revolution," in John W. Lewis, ed., *Party Leadership and Revolutionary Power in China* (Cambridge, Eng.: Cambridge University Press, 1970); and

Frederick C. Teiwes, "The 'Rules of the Game' in Chinese Politics," *Problems of Communism*, Vol. 28, Nos. 5–6 (Sep–Dec 1979):67–76.

6. Michel Oksenberg, "Policy-Making Under Mao, 1949–1968: An overview," in John Lindbeck, ed., *China: Management of a Revolutionary Society* (Seattle: University of Washington Press, 1971); Frederick Teiwes, "Chinese Politics, 1949–1965: A Changing Mao," *Current Scene*, Vol. 12, Nos. 1 and 2 (Jan and Feb 1974):1–15 and 1–18. See also the major work in two volumes by Roderick MacFarquhar, *The Origins of the Cultural Revolution* (New York: Columbia University Press, 1974 and 1983).

7. E.g., William Whitson, "The Concept of Military Generation," *Asian Survey*, Vol. 7, No. 11 (Nov 1968):921–47.

8. Although the factional approach was very widely employed in Hong Kong and Taiwan analyses of mainland affairs, the chief American exponent has been Lucian Pye, as in his *The Dynamics of Chinese Politics* (Cambridge, Mass.: Oelgeschlager, Gunn and Hain, 1981). See also, however, Andrew Nathan, "A Factional Model for Chinese Politics," *China Quarterly*, No. 53 (Jan–Mar 1973):34–66; the critique of Nathan's model in Tang Tsou, "Prolegomenon to the Study of Informal Groups in CCP Politics," *China Quarterly*, No. 65 (Jan–Mar 1976):98–113, and Nathan's reply in the same issue. Also, William Parish, "Factions in Chinese Military Politics," *China Quarterly*, No. 56 (1973):667–99.

9. Much inspiration came from Graham T. Allison, *Essence of Decision: Explaining the Cuban Missile Crisis* (Boston: Little, Brown, 1971).

10. E.g., William Whitson, "Organizational Perspectives and Decision-Making in the Chinese Communist High Command," in Robert Scalapino, ed., *Elites in the People's Republic of China* (Seattle: University of Washington Press, 1972); Frederick Teiwes, "Provincial Politics in China: Themes and Variations," in John Lindbeck, ed., *China: Management of a Revolutionary Society*; and David Bachman, "To Leap Forward: Chinese Policy-Making, 1956–57," Ph.D. diss., Stanford University, 1983.

11. Richard P. Suttmeier, *Research and Revolution: Science Policy and Social Change in China* (Lexington, Mass.: Lexington Books, 1974); June T. Dreyer, *China's Forty Millions: Minority Nationalities and National Integration in the PRC* (Cambridge, Mass.: Harvard University Press, 1976); Thomas P. Bernstein, *Up to the Mountains and Down to the Villages* (New Haven, Conn.: Yale University Press, 1977); Stephen Andors, *China's Industrial Revolution: Politics, Planning and Management* (New York: Pantheon, 1977); David M. Lampton, *The Politics of Medicine in China: The Policy Process 1949–1977* (Boulder,

Col.: Westview, 1977); Benedict Stavis, *The Politics of Agricultural Mechanization* (Ithaca, N.Y.: Cornell University Press, 1978); Lynn T. White, *Careers in Shanghai* (Berkeley: University of California Press, 1978); Harry Harding, *Organizing China: The Problem of Bureaucracy, 1949–1976* (Stanford, Calif.: Stanford University Press, 1981); and Dorothy Solinger, *Chinese Business Under Socialism: The Politics of Domestic Commerce, 1949–1980* (Berkeley: University of California Press, 1984). There were also numerous shorter studies of policy in the areas of education, culture, and the arts.

12. The term was derived from Franklyn Griffiths, "A Tendency Analysis of Soviet Policy-Making," in H. Gordon Skilling and Franklyn Griffiths, eds., *Interest Groups in Soviet Politics* (Princeton, N.J.: Princeton University Press, 1971).

13. Compare, e.g., the parameters of policy groupings employed in such studies as Jack Gray, "The Two Roads: Alternative Strategies of Social Change and Economic Growth in China," in Stuart Schram, ed., *Authority, Participation and Cultural Change in China*; Edward Friedman, "Maoism, Titoism, Stalinism: Some Origins and Consequences of the Maoist Theory of the Socialist Transition," in Mark Selden and Victor Lippit, eds., *The Transition to Socialism in China* (Armonk, N.Y.: M. E. Sharpe, 1982); Maurice Meisner, *Mao's China* (New York: Free Press, 1977); Byung-joon Ahn, *Chinese Politics and the Cultural Revolution* (Seattle: University of Washington Press, 1976); Parris Chang, *Power and Policy in China* (University Park: Pennsylvania State University Press, 1975); Dorothy Solinger, *Chinese Business Under Socialism*; and David Bachman, "To Leap Forward."

14. Zhongnanhai is the government park in Beijing, adjacent to the Forbidden City, where Mao and other leaders had their offices and residences.

15. A major conference of China politics specialists was convened in Ann Arbor in 1977 with this as its premise. Although no volume of conference papers was published, the conference had its impact on the work and the thinking of a number of researchers.

16. Michel Oksenberg, "Occupational Groups in Chinese Society and the Cultural Revolution," in M. Oksenberg *et al.*, *The Cultural Revolution: 1967 in Review*, Michigan Papers in Chinese Studies, No. 2 (Ann Arbor: Center for Chinese Studies, University of Michigan, 1968); Alan P. Liu, *Political Culture and Group Conflict in Communist China* (Santa Barbara, Calif.: ABC-Clio, 1976); and David S. G. Goodman, ed., *Groups and Politics in the People's Republic of China* (Armonk, N.Y.: M. E. Sharpe, 1984.) Although not a study of interest groups *per se*, Hong Yung Lee's fine Cultural Revolution study adopts a similar so-

ciety-based focus for his political analysis: *The Politics of the Chinese Cultural Revolution* (Berkeley: University of California Press, 1978).

17. See the important study by Barry Naughton, "The Decline of Central Control Over Investment," in David M. Lampton, ed., *Policy Implementation in Post-Mao China* (forthcoming). Also, Christine Wong, "The Local Industrial Sector in Post-Mao Reforms," (unpub. ms., Oct 1983); Christine Wong, "Rural Industrialization in the People's Republic of China: Lessons from the Cultural Revolution Decade," in Joint Economic Committee Selected Papers, *China under the Four Modernizations*, Part I (Washington, D.C.: Government Printing Office, 1982):394–418; and Vivienne Shue, "Beyond the Budget: Finance Organization and Reform in a Chinese County," *Modern China*, Vol. 10, No. 2 (1984):147–86.

18. This theme is emphasized in an important forthcoming collection of essays, David M. Lampton, ed., *Policy Implementation in Post-Mao China*. It is also one of the general topics in Vivienne Shue, *Peasant China in Transition* (Berkeley: University of California Press, 1980).

19. See Frederick Teiwes, "'The Rules of the Game.'" A deliberate sequencing and synthesis of approaches is the synoptic recommendation offered in Harry Harding, "Competing Models of the Chinese Communist Policy Process: Toward a Sorting and Evaluation," *Issues and Studies*, Vol. 20, No. 2 (Feb 1984):13–36. I have relied much on Harding's work in assembling this overview of approaches. See, in addition, Harry Harding, "The Study of Chinese Politics: Toward a Third Generation of Scholarship," *World Politics*, Vol. 36, No. 2 (Jan 1984):284–307, where Teiwes's synthesis is also discussed.

20. On statist as opposed to pluralist approaches to the study of politics, see the very helpful review essay by Stephen D. Krasner, "Approaches to the State: Alternative Conceptions and Historical Dynamics," *Comparative Politics*, (Jan 1984):223–46. On politics as allocation, as opposed to politics as "us against them," see Gianfranco Poggi, *The Development of the Modern State* (Stanford, Calif.: Stanford University Press, 1978), ch. 1.

21. The last decade has seen such rapid progress, however, in studies of popular culture and popular protest by social historians, sociologists, and political scientists of Europe and other parts of the world that we should find no shortage of excellent points of departure for this work. Some pioneering attempts have already been made in the contemporary China literature, for example in the works of Elizabeth J. Perry, "Rural Collective Violence: The Fruits of Recent Reforms," in Elizabeth Perry and Christine Wong, eds., *The Political Economy of Reform in Post-Mao China* (Cambridge, Mass.: Harvard University Press, 1985); and

Ann S. Anagnost, "The Beginning and End of an Emperor: A Counter-representation of the State," *Modern China*, Vol. 11, No. 2 (Apr 1985):147−76. See also Ann S. Anagnost, "Politics and Magic in Contemporary China," *Modern China*, Vol. 13, No. 1 (Jan 1987):40−61, along with the other essays in that special issue of *Modern China*.

22. One of the exceptions here would be Kay Ann Johnson, *Women, the Family and Peasant Revolution in China* (Chicago: University of Chicago Press, 1983).

23. This was one of the themes in my own work on policy and the local politics of collectivization in the 1950s however. And this line of inquiry has been pushed forward with encouraging results in two recent works by sociologists: Richard Madsen, *Morality and Power in a Chinese Village* (Berkeley: University of California Press, 1984); and Andrew G. Walder, *Communist Neo-Traditionalism: Work and Authority in Chinese Industry* (Berkeley: University of California Press, 1986).

24. Martin K. Whyte, *Small Groups and Political Rituals in China* (Berkeley: University of California Press, 1974).

25. William L. Parish and Martin K. Whyte, *Village and Family in Contemporary China* (Chicago: University of Chicago Press, 1978), p. 337.

26. E. P. Thompson, *The Poverty of Theory and Other Essays* (New York: Monthly Review Press, 1978), p. 111.

27. For a recent interpretation that emphasizes the remnant feudal aspects of Chinese society under Mao, see William Hinton, *Shenfan* (New York: Random House, 1983). For an interpretation that invokes both feudalism and fascism as appropriate terms of analysis, see Edward Friedman, "The Societal Obstacle to China's Socialist Transition: State Capitalism or Feudal Fascism," in Victor Nee and David Mozingo, eds., *State and Society in Contemporary China*. Friedman explicitly rejects the concept of totalitarianism in analyses of what he prefers to call "Leninist" states because, he argues, it misleadingly implies unchangeability, "a permanent totality." Yet he repeatedly terms the Maoist reign "fascist" (and "feudal") and "murderously malignant." See also Edward Friedman, "Three Leninist Paths Within a Socialist Conundrum," in Dorothy Solinger, ed., *Three Visions of Chinese Socialism* (Boulder, Col.: Westview, 1984). And Tang Tsou, "Back from the Brink of Revolutionary-'Feudal' Totalitarianism," in Nee and Mozingo, eds., *State and Society in Contemporary China*. And compare Peter R. Moody, *Chinese Politics After Mao* (New York: Praeger, 1983).

28. Clifford Geertz, "From the Native's Point of View: On the Nature of Anthropological Understanding," in Geertz, *Local Knowledge* (New York: Basic Books, 1983), p. 69.

29. *Ibid.*

Chapter Two

1. In an elaboration of a faction model of Chinese politics, for example, Lucian Pye has criticized others using the "plural state" approach for exaggerating the role of policy issues in identifying contending political groups. See Lucian W. Pye, *The Dynamics of Factions and Consensus in Chinese Politics* (Santa Monica, Calif.: Rand Corporation, 1980), p. 15.

2. Leon Trotsky, *The Revolution Betrayed* (New York: Pathfinder Press, 1972), p. 112.

3. Trotsky, p. 113.

4. Considerable economic evidence was marshalled to demonstrate the redistributive effects of China's development strategy and its state planning and allocation mechanisms under Mao. See, e.g., Nicholas R. Lardy, "Economic Planning and Income Distribution in China," *Current Scene*, Vol. 14, No. 11 (Nov 1976):1–12; and the detailed study of China's fiscal system, Nicholas R. Lardy, *Economic Growth and Distribution in China* (New York: Cambridge University Press, 1978).

5. For an excellent study of the relevant aspects of Mao Zedong's political thought, see John Bryan Starr, *Continuing the Revolution* (Princeton, N.J.: Princeton University Press, 1979). Also, Edward Friedman, "The Innovator," in Dick Wilson, ed., *Mao Tsetung in the Scales of History* (Cambridge, Eng.: Cambridge University Press, 1977).

6. See, e.g., Bettelheim's assessment in Charles Bettelheim and Neil Burton, *China Since Mao* (New York: Monthly Review Press, 1978).

7. One exception to this rule is David M. Lampton's very interesting work on China's health care policy process. See his *Health, Conflict and the Chinese Political System*, Michigan Papers in Chinese Studies, No. 18 (Ann Arbor: Center for Chinese Studies, 1974).

8. Major theoretical conceptualizations of the relations of "center" and "periphery" are very divergent. Compare the functional sociology approach of Edward Shils, *Center and Periphery: Essays in Macrosociology* (Chicago: University of Chicago Press, 1975); the world political economy approach, of which the *locus classicus* is Immanuel Wallerstein, *The Modern World System* (New York: Academic Press, 1976); the related "internal colonialism" approach, e.g., Alvin W. Gouldner, "Stalinism: A Study of Internal Colonialism," *Telos* (1978):5–48; and the bureaucratic organization approach, e.g., Michel Crozier, *The Bureaucratic Phenomenon* (Chicago: University of Chicago Press, 1964). Sidney Tarrow, in his fine comparative study of French and Italian local politics, provides an overview and critique of these major center-periphery approaches and attempts to formulate a less tendentious synthesis. His own work ultimately turns on bureaucratic-structural linkages,

however. See his *Between Center and Periphery: Grassroots Politicians in Italy and France* (New Haven, Conn.: Yale University Press, 1977), esp. ch. 1. The closest thing to the approach adopted in this essay already applied to China—but to urban China—has been Lynn T. White's superb analyses of the Shanghai polity. See his *Careers in Shanghai* (Berkeley: University of California Press, 1978), and his numerous articles.

9. Shils, p. 9.

10. Tarrow, p. 32.

11. Shils, pp. 80, 81.

12. Harumi Befu, "The Political Relation of the Village to the State," *World Politics*, Vol. 19, No. 4 (Jul 1967):601–20. Befu's article is selected for discussion not because it was unusually important or written with special pertinence to China, but because it is a rigorous and thoughtful piece of work, conceived firmly within the mainstream of the "modernization" paradigm, which happens to address more succinctly and directly than most such works the village-state relationship that is the focus of our concern here.

13. "Centralized chiefdoms" is Eisenstadt's terminology. Befu's debt to Eisenstadt is apparent in most of his constructions and formulations. The other quotations are from Befu, pp. 602 and 603.

14. Quotations characterizing the "classical" and the "modern" state are from Befu, pp. 607, 615, 619.

15. Befu, p. 601. This belief that the Chinese state, during Mao's lifetime, was among the most intrusive in the world, penetrating effectively to control even the most personal aspects of peasant village life, has been very widespread. See, e.g., C. K. Yang, *Chinese Communist Society: The Family and the Village*, Part II (Cambridge, Mass.: MIT Press, 1959), pp. 174–75.

16. On the central domination of model villages, see Edward Friedman, "The Politics of Local Models, Social Transformation and State Power Struggles in the People's Republic of China: Tachai and Teng Hsiao-p'ing," *China Quarterly*, No. 76 (Dec 1978):873–90. For some accounts of the political, social, and economic authority usually retained within nonmodel village communities, see John P. Burns, "The Election of Production Team Cadres in Rural China: 1958–74," *China Quarterly*, No. 74 (Jun 1978):273–96; William L. Parish and Martin King Whyte, *Village and Family in Contemporary China* (Chicago: University of Chicago Press, 1978); and John C. Pelzel, "Economic Management of a Production Brigade in Post-Leap China," in W. E. Willmott, ed., *Economic Organization in Chinese Society* (Stanford, Calif.: Stanford University Press, 1972), esp. p. 398. On cadre-peasant collusion to

evade state demands, see also Thomas P. Bernstein, "Cadre and Peasant Behavior under Conditions of Insecurity and Deprivation: The Grain Supply Crisis of the Spring of 1955," in A. Doak Barnett, ed., *Chinese Communist Politics in Action* (Seattle: University of Washington Press, 1969).

17. Befu, pp. 617, 618. Emphasis added.

18. See, e.g., Talcott Parsons, "The Distribution of Power in American Society," *World Politics*, Vol. 10 (1957):123–43; and, from a different perspective, Nicos Poulantzas, *Political Power and Social Classes* (London: NLB, 1975), pp. 118–19.

19. Vivienne Shue, *Peasant China in Transition: The Dynamics of Development toward Socialism, 1949–1956* (Berkeley: University of California Press, 1980), esp. pp. 342–43.

20. This line of argument is developed somewhat further in this volume's final essay.

21. Befu, pp. 615, 619. See also Shils, *Center and Periphery*, ch. 5. For an intelligent discussion of problems in the sociology of state socialist systems, see also David Lane, *The Socialist Industrial State* (London: Allen and Unwin, 1976), esp. ch. 2.

22. Some of the earlier assessments to the contrary notwithstanding, such as Jack M. Potter, "From Peasants to Rural Proletarians: Social and Economic Change in Rural Communist China," in Jack M. Potter, May N. Diaz, and George M. Foster, eds., *Peasant Society: A Reader* (Boston: Little Brown, 1967), pp. 407–19. More recent studies of Chinese rural life, based largely on émigré interviews, have stressed the continuities and adaptations of traditional peasant social and cultural patterns during the Mao years. See, e.g., William Parish, "Socialism and the Chinese Peasant Family," *Journal of Asian Studies*, Vol. 34 (May 1975):613–30; and Parish and Whyte, *Village and Family in Contemporary China*.

23. A recent article by an anthropologist working in Guangdong Province gives the most comprehensive demonstration of this sharp rural-urban bifurcation of Chinese society. See Sulamith Heins Potter, "The Position of Peasants in Modern China's Social Order," *Modern China*, Vol. 9, No. 4 (Oct 1983):465–99. On some related problems, see D. Gordon White, "The Politics of Hsia-Hsiang Youth," *China Quarterly*, No. 59 (1974):491–517; and Thomas P. Bernstein, *Up to the Mountains and Down to the Villages* (New Haven, Conn.: Yale University Press, 1977), esp. chs. 3 and 4.

24. See Parish, "Socialism and the Chinese Peasant Family"; and Parish and Whyte, *Village and Family*, pp. 95, 321, and *passim*.

25. G. William Skinner, "Marketing and Social Structure in Rural China," Part III, *Journal of Asian Studies*, Vol. 24 (May 1965):363–99.

26. G. William Skinner, "Chinese Peasants and the Closed Community: An Open and Shut Case," *Comparative Studies in Society and History*, Vol. 13 (Jul 1971): 272.

27. Leon H. Mayhew, "Society," *International Encyclopedia of the Social Sciences* (1968), p. 585.

28. Quoted in Teodor Shanin, *The Awkward Class* (Oxford, Eng.: Clarendon Press, 1972), p. 207. For a stimulating discussion of traditional Chinese peasant society relevant to these issues, see Leon Stover, *The Cultural Ecology of Chinese Civilization: Peasants and Elites in the Last of the Agrarian States* (New York: Pica Press, 1974).

29. Hamza Alavi, "Peasant Classes and Primordial Loyalties," *Journal of Peasant Studies*, Vol. 1 (Oct 1973): 37. Alavi was writing about peasantries in capitalist states, but these remarks are relevant to encapsulating socialist states as well.

30. The discussion in this essay should be regarded therefore, as related, but not contributing to, the debate about the relatively "open" or "closed corporate" nature of peasant communities. Cf. Eric R. Wolf, "Closed Corporate Peasant Communities in Meso-america and Central Java," *Southwestern Journal of Anthropology*, Vol. 13 (Spr 1971): 1–18; Eric R. Wolf, "Types of Latin American Peasantry: A Preliminary Discussion," *American Anthropologist*, Vol. 57 (Jun 1955): 452–71; and, on China, G. William Skinner, "Chinese Peasants and the Closed Community."; and the critique of Skinner's hypothesis, A. Terry Rambo, "Closed Corporate and Open Peasant Communities: Reopening a Hastily Shut Case," *Comparative Studies in Society and History*, Vol. 19, No. 2 (1977): 179–88.

31. Shanin, pp. 39, 177.

32. V.I. Lenin, *On the Socialist Transformation of Agriculture* (Moscow: Novosti Press Agency, 1973), pp. 112–13, original emphasis; and p. 161.

33. Franz Schurmann, *Ideology and Organization in Communist China* (Berkeley: University of California Press, 1966), ch. 3, esp. p. 175.

34. *Ibid.*, p. 219.

35. The criss-crossed structure of local government administration and finance is explored in more detail in Vivienne Shue, "Beyond the Budget: Finance Organization and Reform in a Chinese County," *Modern China*, Vol. 10, No. 2 (1984): 147–86.

36. This pattern was more prominent in the administration of rural areas. Urban areas, as Schurmann pointed out, "rely more on [vertical] departments and bureaux rather than on [horizontal] committees—undoubtedly because cities are easier to rule bureaucratically than urban areas." Schurmann, p. 212.

37. This old Maoist emphasis on the locally bounded but internally

diversified rural economy tends to be forgotten now in the glare of publicity about the economic diversification that has come to the countryside with local specialization and market integration under the Deng Xiaoping reforms of the 1980s.

38. Audrey Donnithorne, "China's Cellular Economy: Some Economic Trends Since the Cultural Revolution," *China Quarterly*, No. 52 (1972):605–19.

39. E.g., Dwight Perkins *et al.*, *Rural Small-Scale Industry in the People's Republic of China* (Berkeley: University of California Press, 1977); Carl Riskin, "Small Industry and the Chinese Model of Development," *China Quarterly*, No. 46 (Jun 1971):245–73; and Jon Sigurdson, "Rural Industry and the Internal Transfer of Technology," in Stuart Schram, ed., *Authority, Participation and Cultural Change in China*, (Cambridge, Eng.: Cambridge University Press, 1973), pp. 199–232.

40. On the tortuous complexity and contingency of the process of transforming peasant culture into socialist culture as the CCP understood that process early on, see Vivienne Shue, "Peasant Culture and Socialist Culture in China: On the Dynamics of Structure, Behavior, and Value Change in Socialist Systems," in Godwin Chu and Francis Hsu, eds., *Moving a Mountain: Cultural Change in China* (Honolulu: University of Hawaii Press, 1979), pp. 305–40.

41. William L. Parish, "Communication and Changing Rural Life," in Chu and Hsu, eds., *Moving a Mountain*, p. 380.

42. *Ibid.*, p. 381.

43. Shue, *Peasant China in Transition*, pp. 323–24. See also Thomas P. Bernstein, "Leadership and Mass Mobilisation in the Soviet and Chinese Collectivisation Campaigns of 1929–30 and 1955–56: A Comparison," *China Quarterly*, No. 31 (1967):1–47.

44. This was the unanimous finding of several different research projects based on émigré accounts in the 1970s. One informant from rural Guangdong told me, e.g.: "Very many people did not want to be team leader. The team leader only got a supplement of a few hundred workpoints a year, but he had to take on a certain amount of responsibility and trouble. If things went well, then most people would be satisfied and think there was no problem. But there would still be a few who would be dissatisfied and they would curse you. And because the team leader had to take responsibility for every little affair that came up in the team, he had less time for his own private plot and for tending to his own family affairs. So, most people were not willing to be team leader." Shue, Hong Kong Interview Series:78, CTS, 8. See also, Parish and Whyte, *Village and Family*, pp. 106–7; and B. Michael Frolic, *Mao's People* (Cambridge, Mass.: Harvard University Press, 1980), pp. 31–32.

45. This thought had its origin in reading Clifford Geertz, "The Inte-

grative Revolution: Primordial Sentiments and Civil Politics in the New States," in Clifford Geertz, ed., *Old Societies and New States* (New York: Free Press, 1963), esp. p. 128.

Chapter Three

1. On "first" and "second" wave reforms, see Vivienne Shue, "The New Course in Chinese Agriculture," *The Annals* (of the American Academy of Political and Social Scientists), No. 476 (Nov 1984):74–88.

2. *Ibid.* On the details of "the separation of government and economy" in people's communes, see also Vivienne Shue, "The Fate of the Commune," *Modern China*, Vol. 10, No. 3 (Jul 1984):259–83.

3. Both "fascist" and "feudal"?—to put the question in the Li Yizhe categories now widely employed in China. For the critical philosophy of the Li Yizhe group, see the convenient collection by Anita Chan, Stanley Rosen, and Jonathan Unger, eds., *On Socialist Democracy and the Chinese Legal System* (Armonk, N.Y.: M. E. Sharpe, 1985).

4. A more recent and growing body of revisionist scholarship in Japan and the West has been challenging this historical indictment of the gentry, however, as noted below.

5. Mark Elvin, *The Pattern of the Chinese Past* (Stanford, Calif.: Stanford University Press, 1973), p. 23. See also, Hsu Cho-yun, *Ancient China in Transition* (Stanford, Calif.: Stanford University Press, 1965), esp. pp. 92–106.

6. Elvin, *The Pattern*, pp. 21–22.

7. *Ibid.* pp. 29–30.

8. *Ibid.* p. 34.

9. Patricia Ebrey, *The Aristocratic Families of Early Imperial China* (Cambridge, Eng.: Cambridge University Press, 1978), p. 118.

10. *Ibid.* p. 2.

11. On the survival of Han imperial institutions, and thus the inappropriateness of comparison with the breakdown of the Roman Empire, see also the brief but interesting remarks in Witold Rodzinski, *The Walled Kingdom* (New York: Free Press, 1984), p. 67.

12. Denis Twitchett, *Financial Administration under the T'ang Dynasty* (Cambridge, Eng.: Cambridge University Press, 1962), pp. 1–6.

13. Denis Twitchett, *Land Tenure and the Social Order in T'ang and Sung China* (London: 1964), p. 25 and *passim*.

14. On the growing importance of the examinations in the selection of new officials during the Song, see E. A. Kracke, Jr., *Civil Service in Early Sung China* (Cambridge, Mass.: Harvard University Press, 1953), esp. ch. 4. Even during the Song, however, the relative rise in importance of the professional scholar elite, as opposed to local landed families, may have been neither steady nor ineluctable. See Robert Hartwell, "Demo-

graphic, Political, and Social Transformations of China, 750–1550," *Harvard Journal of Asiatic Studies*, Vol. 42, No. 2 (1982):365–442, esp. pp. 405–25. Whether or not one is persuaded by Hartwell's account, it is obvious that the general social trends of necessity rather brutally summarized here were always marked by tension, struggle, and indeterminacy.

15. It includes only "officials, active, retired, expectant, and potential; subofficials, *chin-shih*, *chu-jen*, *kung-sheng*, both regular and irregular [i.e., in most cases, purchased]; and *chien-sheng* [a purchased degree]." For the Qing, Ho even excludes the *chien-sheng*. Yet in small places, and especially in rural villages, even the relatively less accomplished *sheng-yuan* were often regarded as men of stature and influence well beyond that of ordinary commoners. Ho Ping-ti, *The Ladder of Success in Imperial China* (New York: Columbia University Press, 1962), pp. 38, 40.

16. That is, *chin-shih*, *chu-jen*, and *kung-sheng*. Chang Chung-li, *The Chinese Gentry* (Seattle: University of Washington Press, 1955), pp. 6ff.

17. Frederic Wakeman, *The Fall of Imperial China* (New York: Free Press, 1975), p. 25. The internal stratification of the gentry went even further than this, of course. At various periods, northern and southern gentry differed markedly and pursued different interests. During the Qing, distinctions might be made between Manchu and Han gentry groups, and so on. Note that all three definitional schemes cited here are derived from the social conditions of the Ming-Qing era only. For more interesting work on stratification of local elites in the late Ming, see Jerry Dennerline, *The Chia-ting Loyalists* (New Haven, Conn: Yale University Press, 1981), esp. chs. 3 and 4. Aspects of gentry composition at earlier epochs must, only for lack of knowledge on my part, remain outside the scope of this essay. For very helpful discussions of the nature and political behavior of China's local elites at later periods, however, see, e.g., R. Keith Schoppa, *Chinese Elites and Political Change* (Cambridge, Mass.: Harvard University Press, 1982); and John H. Fincher, *Chinese Democracy: The Self-Government Movement in Local Provincial and National Politics, 1905–1914* (New York: St. Martin's Press, 1981).

18. Or, as Philip Huang has elaborated so well on this important pattern: "What the late imperial Chinese state did was to resort in the main to an indirect means of control, attempting to secure the loyalty of the village elites by holding before them the possibility of entering the upper tier through the well-controlled examination system. In short, what connected and held together the two tiers of this sociopolitical system were the avenues of mobility that gave commoner elites access to the gentry elites, that allowed rich peasants, managerial farmers, and landlords to become gentry landlords and officials. Those avenues lent flexibility and

vitality to the Qing system." Philip C. C. Huang, *The Peasant Economy and Social Change in North China* (Stanford, Calif.: Stanford University Press, 1985), p. 248.

19. Etienne Balazs, *Chinese Civilization and Bureaucracy* (New Haven, Conn.: Yale University Press, 1964), pp. 20–21. See also pp. 30 and 169.

20. Albert Feuerwerker, *State and Society in Eighteenth Century China* (Ann Arbor, Mich.: Center for Chinese Studies, 1976), pp. 19, 21 (emphasis added).

21. See also the neat summary and comments on this issue in Theda Skocpol, *States and Social Revolutions* (New York: Cambridge University Press, 1979), p. 72.

22. In the company of some American historians of China these days, just to propose making a comparison between Western and Chinese paths to the present is enough to provoke winces of intellectual pain, cries of teleological "foul play," and grumbles about the ineradicable ethnocentricity of Western scholarship. After repeated bouts with Weberian, Marxian, and "modernization theory" paradigms, all of which (but each for different reasons) depicted China's old society as unwholesomely backward, China's old economy as flaccidly underdeveloped, and China's whole history as amazingly and endlessly static, these scholars are leery of comparisons. They believe the whole tradition-modernity dichotomy is biased and bankrupt and they are tired of unilinear stages-of-development models that inevitably stack the analytical deck against appreciation of Chinese achievements. They demand a history of China written in her own terms. See, e.g., Paul A. Cohen, *Discovering History in China* (New York: Columbia University Press, 1984). But just to *speak* of "modernity" is not (anymore) to praise it. And to make comparisons with Western history and culture need not be to disparage Chinese differentness. Some anthropologists and numerous young social historians of China are now finding ways to make pertinent, sophisticated, and balanced use of comparative social theory in their work. We must learn to choose our theoretical categories and our social indicators very carefully, of course. But in the long run, prudent comparison holds more promise of genuine understanding than attitudes and approaches that dwell on Chinese exceptionalism.

23. It is possible to overstrain this contrast. As Ben Anderson has pointed out to me, it must not be forgotten that European culture under feudalism remained profoundly united by Christianity, Latin, the spirit of diplomacy, and Grotius's "international law." The pattern of European statemaking owes much to that special combination of cultural unity and political fragmentation characteristic of the Middle Ages.

24. Charles Tilly, "Reflections on the History of European State-

Making," in Charles Tilly, ed., *The Formation of National States in Western Europe* (Princeton, N.J.: Princeton University Press, 1975), pp. 24–25.

25. See Ira Katznelson, *City Trenches*, (New York: Pantheon, 1981), pp. 29–31.

26. Perry Anderson, *Lineages of the Absolutist State* (London: NLB, 1974), p. 21.

27. *Ibid*. p. 18.

28. *Ibid*. p. 41.

29. But for a different view of the special role of the large urban complexes like Antwerp, Geneva, Amsterdam, and Genoa, see Fernand Braudel, *The Wheels of Commerce* (New York: Harper, 1979): 518–22, 532–37, and *passim*. Braudel makes it clear that the Pope and monarchs like Louis XI and Charles V, whose tax revenues were chronically insufficient, were continually borrowing enormous sums from bankers and other backers at home and abroad. Philip II repeatedly went bankrupt to "superior financier[s] of international standing." Braudel's picture, therefore, is not necessarily that of a pleasant harmony of interests between the wealthy urban bourgeoisie and the state. On many occasions the absolutists found themselves dictated to by the money czars of those great cities.

30. Jacques Gernet, *Le Monde Chinois* (Paris: Colin, 1972), pp. 238–39. My translation.

31. Balazs, p. 78.

32. William T. Rowe, *Hankow: Commerce and Society in a Chinese City, 1796–1889* (Stanford, Calif.: Stanford University Press, 1984), p. 11.

33. *Ibid*., pp. 344–45 and 339 (emphasis added). Note that this aspect of Rowe's argument is quite congruent with the general approach to Chinese state-society analysis adopted here.

34. Rowe himself notes the continued, even enhanced, interpenetration of the commercial and bureaucratic elite spheres saying, "in the late Ch'ing more and more merchants became officials and officials, merchants" (p. 204). Hankou merchants continued buying ranks and degrees, thus transmuting their wealth into social status of the old sort. Rowe estimates that in the late 1800s "more than half the city's brokers and major wholesale dealers had such status" (p. 207). True, the ranks and degrees brought these families certain practical immunities from punishment, but only at the cost of acquiescing in the ancient Chinese social status system, which regarded merchants and moneymaking as lowly. And on a related phenomenon, Rowe can only comment rather lamely that "For any number of reasons, officials acting as private entrepreneurs in Hankow preferred to conceal their investments" (p. 205). In

very important ways, it seems, the social value system of the past sur-vived, despite the rise of an urban identity as such. See also, Marie-Claire Bergère, "The Chinese Bourgeoisie, 1911–1937," in Denis Twitchett and John K. Fairbank, eds., *The Cambridge History of China*, Vol. 12, Part 1 (Cambridge, Eng.: Cambridge University Press, 1983), esp. pp. 722–27.

35. It should be noted that Rowe quite clearly does not claim that the Hankou milieu he describes can, or should, be labeled "capitalist." In his concluding chapter, where he states his leading hypotheses most broadly, he reminds us that he has been talking about an "incipient" bourgeoisie and suggests tentatively only (in the future conditional) that "China would, if left to itself, ultimately have developed into an indus-trial capitalist society comparable to that of the West" (p. 345).

36. In his review of Rowe's book, David Buck, while finding much to praise concludes: "Rowe and others cannot escape the evidence that no matter what the increasing strength[s] of indigenous Chinese urban and bourgeois forces were in the nineteenth century, by the early twentieth century these elements were not strong enough to prevail against suc-cessive combinations of central state authority, military might, modern mass ideologies and political parties, and foreign intervention for con-trol of Chinese society. Moreover, the Chinese urban bourgeoisie and Chinese capitalists still fell far short of Western and Japanese mastery of capitalism's potential for control of finances, transportation, and indus-trial production." Buck's review is in *Journal of Asian Studies*, Vol. 44, No. 4 (Aug 1985):819–21.

37. For another interesting perspective on the commercial roles of the gentry, see Barrington Moore, Jr., *Social Origins of Dictatorship and Democracy* (Boston: Beacon, 1966), pp. 174–78.

38. See, e.g., Endymion Wilkinson, *Landlord and Labor in Late Im-perial China* (Cambridge, Mass.: Harvard University Press, 1978). Also helpful on the urban roles of gentry are several of the essays in G. William Skinner, ed., *The City in Late Imperial China* (Stanford, Calif: Stanford University Press, 1979).

39. Maurice Meisner, *Mao's China* (New York: Free Press, 1977), ch. 1. This assertion is not meant to suggest that we can overlook the role of class-based political action in the final overthrow of the Qing. But the logic and strategy of engineering the Qing collapse, even for those who spoke for particular class interests, was finally to be found in geographical separatism. See Fincher, *Chinese Democracy*; and John Fincher, "Political Provincialism and the National Revolution," in Mary C. Wright, ed., *China in Revolution* (New Haven, Conn.: Yale Univer-sity Press), pp. 185–226. For an alternative formulation of some of the processes involved in the "breakdown of the traditional state," see Philip

A. Kuhn, *Rebellion and Its Enemies in Late Imperial China* (Cambridge, Mass.: Harvard University Press, 1970), esp. pp. 211–25.

40. Fei Hsiao-tung, *China's Gentry* (Chicago: University of Chicago Press, 1953), pp. 83–84.

41. Ch'u T'ung-tsu, *Local Government in China under the Ch'ing* (Stanford, Calif.: Stanford University Press, 1962), pp. 180, 183–84; and Hsiao Kung-chuan, *Rural China: Imperial Control in the Nineteenth Century* (Seattle: University of Washington Press, 1960), pp. 294–95. Please note that this section on the gentry and local governance is based only on studies of the Qing.

42. Ch'u, *Local Government*, p. 162. On various weaknesses of the *xiangyue* system see John R. Watt, *The District Magistrate in Late Imperial China* (New York: Columbia University Press, 1972), esp. pp. 149–51 and 193–96.

43. Sometimes in fact, however, submagistrates were appointed to serve below the county magistrate.

44. Hsiao, *Rural China*, p. 5. This is the estimate for the year 1749.

45. Jerome B. Grieder, *Intellectuals and the State in Modern China* (New York: Free Press, 1981), pp. 15–16.

46. Moore, *Social Origins*, p. 172.

47. For a greater appreciation of the Qing's struggle to cope with the costs of local government, however, see the superb study by Madeleine Zelin, *The Magistrate's Tael: Rationalizing Fiscal Reform in Eighteenth-Century Ch'ing China* (Berkeley: University of California Press, 1984).

48. Hsiao, p. 125. Hsiao's discussion, and Zelin's, show that, where the gentry was concerned, Qing tax policy underwent repeated revisions making the generalizations here accurate in the main but truer (and more problematic) in some periods than in others.

49. Ch'u, p. 186.

50. But again, on the earlier Qing struggle to control tax farming and various forms of corruption, see Zelin, *The Magistrate's Tael.*

51. *Ibid.* p. 187.

52. Hsiao, p. 133.

53. As Philip Huang (p. 231) has concluded, on the basis of his detailed study of Baodi in north China: "The problem of tax collection exposed in these cases suggest[s] that state power penetrated local societies to only a limited degree. In nineteenth-century Baodi, at least, official power certainly came nowhere near to the abstract bureaucratic ideal embodied in the paochia and lichia systems. Nor, for that matter, did it approximate the fallback position of making the local leaders collectively responsible for tax collection. Instead, the Baodi example suggests a kind of equilibrium in power between state and local society, in which taxes could generally only be levied to the extent that local lead-

ers and village communities considered tolerable." Note how Huang's formulation employing the notion of an equilibrium resembles Feuerwerker's model of the state-society relationship referred to above.

54. See Ch'u, pp. 189–90; Hsiao, pp. 318–20.

55. Ch'u, p. 190.   56. *Ibid.*, pp. 172–73.

57. Hsiao, p. 317.   58. *Ibid.*, p. 320.

59. The civil service examination system itself had been abolished in 1905. For some debate on the degree to which gentry ambitions and strategies were altered after 1900, see Chuzo Ichiko, "The Role of the Gentry: An Hypothesis," in Mary Wright, ed., *China in Revolution*, and Wright's comments in the editor's introduction, pp. 39–40. See also Kuhn, *Rebellion*, p. 217n.

60. See, e.g., Philip A. Kuhn, "Local Self-Government under the Republic," in Frederic Wakeman and Carolyn Grant, eds., *Conflict and Control in Late Imperial China* (Berkeley: University of California Press, 1975), pp. 257–98. Also, the works by John Fincher and R. Keith Schoppa cited above, and Robert E. Bedeski, *State-Building in Modern China: The Kuomintang in the Prewar Period* (Berkeley, Calif.: Center for Chinese Studies, 1981) (China Research Monograph No. 18).

61. On the scope of county budgets and their relation to commune finance, see Vivienne Shue, "Beyond the Budget: Finance Organization and Reform in a Chinese County," *Modern China*, Vol. 10, No. 2 (Apr 1984):147–86.

62. Hong Kong Interview Series (HKIS):78, CYT 3/2, 63. This and all other interview extracts are from a series of conversations I conducted with Guangdong émigrés in Hong Kong in 1978.

63. HKIS:78, LZC 1/1, 19.

64. *Ibid.*, LZC 1/1, 10–11.

65. *Ibid.*, LZC 1/1, 12–13.

66. Much recent research confirms this general pattern. See, e.g., Jean C. Oi, *State and Peasant in Contemporary China*, forthcoming, and David Zweig, "Agrarian Radicalism in China, 1968–1978: The Search for a Social Base," Ph.D. diss., University of Michigan, 1983. And also Richard Madsen, *Morality and Power in a Chinese Village* (Berkeley: University of California Press, 1984).

67. HKIS:78, CXC 1/1, 19.

68. See, e.g., Anita Chan, Richard Madsen, and Jonathan Unger, *Chen Village* (Berkeley: University of California Press, 1984), which is richly illustrative and instructive on the different styles and goals of village cadres. See also Madsen, *Morality and Power*.

69. HKIS:78, GSJ 2/2, 35.

70. The readiness with which team and even brigade cadres often re-

signed their troublesome and not very lucrative positions has been frequently noted by students of recent Chinese politics.

71. Franz Schurmann, *Ideology and Organization in Communist China* (Berkeley: University of California Press, 1966), p. 416.

72. And in today's more liberal atmosphere, where a wider variety of lifestyles and personal satisfactions is permitted, it seems not so much the state as the party and its austere "serve the people" value system that is threatened by this reform.

73. Shue, "The Fate of the Commune."

74. Martin King Whyte, "Society," in Steven M. Goldstein, ed., *China Briefing, 1984* (Boulder, Col.: Westview, 1985), p. 38.

Chapter Four

1. See the interview with Hu Yaobang reported in Daniel Southerland, "Party Leader Says China To Extend Economic Reform," *Washington Post*, Sep 24, 1986.

2. At the very beginning, of course, the "gang of four" was reviled as "ultra-rightist." For a detailed explanation, see William A. Joseph, *The Critique of Ultra-Leftism in China, 1958–1981* (Stanford, Calif.: Stanford University Press, 1984), esp. ch. 6.

3. For just one of several such heroic attempts, see Merle Goldman and Marshall I. Goldman, "What's New on Peking's Goldfish Lane," *New York Times*, Jul 22, 1986. They write: "It is easy for outsiders to overlook contradictions in China's economic reforms—for the state both encourages private initiative and guides it with a firm hand. For example, in 1985, the Peking municipal administration ordered families living on side streets off main shopping areas to convert their rooms facing the street into private shops. The inhabitants of Goldfish Lane had to conform or move. The increase in nonstate activity was thus mandated by the state."

4. On the limits of "democratization" and other political reforms under Deng see, e.g., James Seymour, "The Abortive Attempt to Democratize China's Political System," in Ronald A. Morse, ed., *The Limits of Reform in China* (Boulder, Col.: Westview, 1983), pp. 139–55; Harry Harding, "Political Development in Post-Mao China," in A. Doak Barnett and Ralph N. Clough, eds., *Modernizing China* (Boulder, Col.: Westview, 1986); and Kevin O'Brien, "Continuity and Change in Chinese Legislative Politics," Ph.D. diss., Yale University, 1986.

5. For relevant discussion, see Merle Goldman, "Culture," in Steven M. Goldstein, ed., *China Briefing, 1984* (Boulder, Col.: Westview, 1985), pp. 21–36; and Perry Link, "Intellectuals and Cultural Policy

after Mao," in Barnett and Clough, eds., *Modernizing China,* pp. 81–102.

6. For administrative purposes, communes were internally broken down into smaller units, territorially defined and with attention to kinship and dwelling patterns. These subdivisions, called "brigades" and "teams" were not only residential, but work-sharing and accounting units.

7. Shulu County Interview Series:79, p. 205.

8. Hong Kong Interview Series (HKIS):78, CYT 2/1, 22.

9. William L. Parish and Martin King Whyte, *Village and Family in Contemporary China* (Chicago: University of Chicago Press, 1978), p. 171.

10. This is one of the major themes of early CCP political style and tactics explored in William Hinton, *Fanshen* (New York: Vintage, 1968). See also Mark Selden, *The Yenan Way in Revolutionary China* (Cambridge, Mass.: Harvard University Press, 1971).

11. On the pressures and the debates leading up to the Great Leap Forward, see Roderick MacFarquhar, *The Origins of the Cultural Revolution,* Vol. 2 (New York: Columbia University Press, 1983).

12. On the campaign itself see Richard Baum and Frederick C. Teiwes, *Ssu-Ch'ing: The Socialist Education Movement of 1962–1966* (Berkeley, Calif.: Center for Chinese Studies, 1968), and Richard Baum, *Prelude to Revolution* (New York: Columbia University Press, 1975). The effects of the campaign on the cadres and people of a Guangdong village are explored in Anita Chan, Richard Madsen and Jonathan Unger, *Chen Village* (Berkeley: University of California Press, 1984).

13. There were political campaigns of esoteric reference, such as the "Water Margin" campaign of 1975; and others that simply seemed unfocused and uncertain in their purpose, such as the campaign to "Criticize Lin Biao and Confucius." All political campaigns were potentially dangerous for cadres, however.

14. The extremely egalitarian "Dazhai workpoint system," propagandized by the center for use in every agricultural production unit in the country, was allowed to lapse out of actual practice in this way. Under central pressure, many units had to agree to try the system for a while. But after a year or two, they quietly dropped back to other, less stringently egalitarian, methods. The official media, however, continued to trumpet the superiority of the system. And since rural units received glorifying press coverage when they agreed to try the Dazhai workpoint regime, but no coverage when they later slipped back into old ways, the impression left abroad was one of much greater local compliance with this "leftist" policy than was in fact the case.

15. All informants in the interview series summarized here were from Guangdong. Conditions may well have varied widely in other provinces in the 1970s.

16. HKIS:78, CTS 1/1, 12.   17. *Ibid.*, CYT 2/2, 30–32.

18. *Ibid.*, CSS 1/1, 17.   19. *Ibid.*, CSS 1/2, 27–28.

20. In Chan, Madsen, and Unger's widely read *Chen Village*, the cadre Longyong is described as fitting this general behavior pattern very closely.

21. See, e.g., Barry Naughton, "The Decline of Central Control Over Investment," in David M. Lampton, ed., *Policy Implementation in Post-Mao China* (University of California Press, forthcoming). Also, Christine Wong, "The Local Industrial Sector in Post-Mao Reforms" (unpub. ms., Oct 1983); Christine Wong, "Rural Industrialization in the People's Republic of China: Lessons from the Cultural Revolution Decade," in Joint Economic Committee Selected Papers, *China under the Four Modernizations*, Part I (Washington, D.C.: Government Printing Office, 1982), pp. 394–418.

22. Details and figures can be found in Vivienne Shue, "Beyond the Budget: Finance Organization and Reform in a Chinese County," *Modern China*, Vol. 10, No. 2 (Apr 1984):147–86.

23. These speculations are based on comparing my notes from in-depth interviews with officials of Shulu county (Hebei) and Wuxi county (Jiangsu) in 1979. In wealthier Wuxi, brigade-level collective entrepreurship was much more pronounced than in Shulu, where the entire county had to be taken as a field for capital accumulation and resource organization for "collective" development. The contrast between the two counties in degree of decentralized development is explored in my unpublished paper, "A Sketch for a Model of Entrepreneurial Arenas in China's Rural Counties: Wuxi and Shulu in the 1970s," Oct 1982.

24. This is an argument made by Richard Madsen in *Morality and Power in a Chinese Village* (Berkeley: University of California Press, 1984).

25. The remainder of this paragraph is based on a most helpful paper by Gordon White, "The Impact of Economic Reforms in the Chinese Countryside: Towards the Politics of Social Capitalism?" (Oct 1985), which is forthcoming in *Modern China*. For more on the rise of new rural economic elites in the last few years, and the possible political consequences, see Daniel R. Kelliher, "State-Peasant Relations under China's Contemporary Reforms," Ph.D. diss., Yale University, 1985.